TINSA

TINSA

A Neurological Approach to the Treatment of Sex Addiction

MICHAEL BARTA PH.D., LPC, CSAT-S

First edition: January 2018
Editor: Marianne Harkin
Cover art: CreateSpace

ISBN 10: 198173869X
ISBN 13: 9781981738694
Library of Congress Control Number: 2017919534
CreateSpace Independent Publishing Platform
North Charleston, South Carolina

Table of Contents

Preface

The intent of this book is to help men who suffer from sex and pornography addictions to achieve long-term recovery by providing access to a model that treats the core of their addictive behaviors rather than relying solely on abstinence-based solutions. Evolving treatments show promise in developing more effective treatment methods as they move away from merely managing symptoms to identifying the causation of addiction. The following pages will help readers to reach a deeper understanding of how a person can become addicted to sexual behaviors. I will explain the neurobiology of addiction and how traumatic developmental wounding can cause abnormalities in the nervous system. Once one is able to uncover the root causes of sex addiction, it is then possible to create an effective path to healing and recovery.

The TINSA (trauma-induced sexual addiction) model was developed after ten years of extensive research in the areas of sex addiction and neuroscience. It is now the primary form of therapy in multiple treatment centers throughout Colorado and has been used in the treatment of over fifteen hundred sex addicts and couples. The TINSA model assumes that the primary origin of sexual addiction lies in a damaged autonomic nervous system (ANS) due to developmental traumas. TINSA contends that early wounding events, such as a lack of attunement and emotional neglect, can predispose a person to addiction by incurring damage to a person's neurological systems.

Although this treatment modality is theoretical in nature, its foundation was built upon more than a decade of empirical evidence put forth by the findings of leaders in their various fields. Stephen Porges, Robert Scaer, Bessel van der Kolk, Patrick Carnes, Bruce Perry, Patricia Ogden, and Peter Levine are all authors and researchers, and many are neuroscientists who have revolutionized therapy and pioneered the way for research in the areas of trauma and behavioral or sex addiction. Their research will be used throughout this text to increase overall understanding of sex addiction and to support the position that this addiction is directly related to adverse experiences that occurred in the human developmental process.

In my findings, the single commonality that sex addicts share is that they were all subjected to developmental trauma. These adverse developmental experiences were the primary cause of their chronic sexually compulsive behaviors. Specifically, the addicts treated in the Colorado centers suffered from the lack of attunement or were invalidated for their authentic worth. Although much research has been done identifying past trauma as a catalyst for addiction, there has not (until now) been a model to apply this knowledge specifically to sex addiction. Contrary to most sex addiction treatment programs that do not fully address the damages done by these early wounding events (or ignore them altogether), the TINSA model proposes that healing and recovery are, in fact, reliant upon exposing the direct link between episodes of past trauma and present behaviors.

Past trauma is not necessarily one particular, catastrophic event. It can be defined as "any event or experience that is physically or psychologically overwhelming to the exposed individual" (Courtois 2014, 12). Trauma can be broken down into many different subtypes; however, interpersonal trauma, such as lack of early parental bonding, will be the primary focus of this text. Early adverse developmental experiences within the family of origin are common among those suffering from sex addiction. These adverse experiences most often occurred in the form of attachment wounds, such as a lack of protection and a lack of attunement. Most addicts suffer from abandonment, neglect, invasion wounding, or oppression; these wounding events each revolved around their not being given a space in which to be authentic or in which to be vulnerable.

Repercussions of childhood trauma such as these can cause a person to seek outside substances and behaviors in an attempt to control one's emotional state. Children are vulnerable and authentic by nature; however, when they are not allowed a space in which to express these innate characteristics, they will begin to form protection mechanisms in an attempt to protect themselves from further emotional suppression. This can incur problematic repercussions, as authenticity and vulnerability are the basic building blocks of intimacy.

There is much research that links addiction to developmental traumas. In fact, a vast number of studies show that addicts of *all* types typically report multiple instances and forms of early-life neglect, abuse, shame, and family dysfunction. The TINSA model theorizes that episodes of past trauma are the *primary* cause in the case of sex addiction. The model also contends that a lack of parental attunement and other adverse developmental events can cause damage to the brain and autonomic nervous system, stunting emotional and psychological growth. This can provoke an individual to seek outside substances or feel-good behaviors in an attempt to regulate this damaged system. When a person is raised in an emotionally vacant home, he or she is then being set up to seek alternative ways of producing dopamine, the main neurotransmitter associated with pleasure in the brain. Since the earliest feel-good behavior that a child often finds is sexual pleasure, masturbation and similar early sexual activity can easily become a go-to source of dopamine and a chosen tool for mood regulation. Over time, however, if this pattern of behavior continues, this acting out can escalate, driven by the need to produce more and more dopamine in order to achieve a comparable "high" each time. If this pattern of behavior continues into adulthood, a person can eventually find him- or herself participating in compulsive, high-risk sexual behaviors that can lead to self-destruction of career, relationships, and personal happiness.

By addressing old wounds and providing the reader with a platform on which to begin trauma treatment, the TINSA model offers a solution for the millions of people suffering from this debilitating disease. It is estimated that 6 to 8 percent of the US population suffers from sexual compulsion disorders, a statistic solely based on the number of individuals who have sought professional help for their disorder (AddictionHope.com 2018). This number is almost certain to be extremely low, as a great many people who partake in uncontrollable and compulsive sexual behaviors do not seek professional help because of the stigma and shame associated with this addiction.

To fully grasp the gravity of this issue, one must carefully consider other research and factors besides a simple head count of those who have enrolled in treatment facilities. There are a number of other warning signs that give us a glimpse of the scope of this dangerous and escalating problem, such as pornography being deemed an "epidemic" by Utah state legislation. There is no doubt that sex addiction is a crisis on the rise, one that negatively impacts millions of lives. To continue to ignore the gravity of this issue only perpetuates the suffering.

Sex addiction is purposeful. It is an attempt to solve leftover problems that linger from early developmental wounding. Unfortunately, the solution eventually stops working and instead becomes the cause of pain, suffering, and humiliation. Sex addiction can lead to divorce, illness, institutionalization, or even death. While the TINSA model can be easily implemented alongside behavioral therapies, my findings have shown that full recovery can only be achieved by addressing the neurological damage done by adverse developmental experiences. When the aforementioned research is combined with the abundant amount of evidence showing that trauma can stifle a person's brain development and function, it is merely a matter of adding the two together. By connecting the statistical and scientific dots, we can now understand exactly how sex addiction occurs and provide a supplementary method for healing. It is our duty as a society to address this epidemic for future generations who are prematurely being given limitless access to online pornography, the great accelerator of this addiction. The TINSA model has proven that when the causes and conditions are treated, the compulsive sexual behaviors become much easier to manage and, in time, become unnecessary.

There is nothing fun about living life as a sex addict. Shame, guilt, extreme self-loathing, and depression are just a few of the internal conflicts that most addicts wrestle with daily. Addicts regularly report dealing with one or more of the following directly related, major life-altering consequences: loss of employment, deterioration of marriage or relationships, and loss of social reputation. It is my hope that by sharing my own personal struggle, thoroughly explaining the TINSA model, and cohesively presenting the large body of evidence that supports neuroscientific research and other statistical data in the field, this book will help sufferers of this disease regain control of their compulsive behaviors and take back their lives. It is also my hope that this book will provide steps to further reduce the stigma associated with this addiction and encourage people to come clean and seek professional help.

This book holds my cumulative life training and educational experience as it pertains to addiction, and in particular, sex addiction. I myself fight the battle found within these pages. I am an addict; however, for over thirty-one years I have done my best to recover with the help of numerous therapists, multiple treatment models, and twelve-step programs. I have made it my life's work to understand addiction, those whom it affects, and recovery solutions in the various forms of training programs, private practice readings, and educational experiences. I have personally, at one time or another, struggled with the very same feelings of inner shame and self-loathing that every addict carries. In 2007, I was living a life completely controlled by impulsive sexual behavior, to the point that it escalated to finding myself in places and with people I could have never imagined. My "rock bottom" included being the center of a sting operation and arrested for solicitation of prostitution, an event that later cost me my job. As a result, I found myself, a highly educated forty-eight-year-old man with a Ph.D, waiting tables for a living.

It was around this time that I entered into a monthlong rehab program for sex addiction and became involved in a local twelve-step program. In my gut, however, I felt that there were still core issues and root causes to my addiction that were not being addressed and wounds that were not yet healed. I began a quest for my own answers and sought training in the field of sex addiction at the International Institute for Trauma and Addiction Professionals (IITAP), the premier training resource for therapists specializing in the treatment of addiction and trauma. I was trained by professionals, including founder Dr. Patrick Carnes, who is widely regarded as the face of sex addiction therapy. It was upon discovering his work that I began to grasp the idea that this was really all about issues that happened early in life. Whereas the twelve steps provided me with abstinence-based ways to control my addiction, I realized that recovery seemed to have a lot more to do with answering the question of why this happened than with simply trying to stay sober. I read the teachings of Peter Levine, Pat Ogden, Stephen Porges, Gabor Maté, and other neurobiologists who assert that developmental childhood trauma and adverse experiences can have profound effects on the brain and lead to compulsive behaviors. When plugging in sex addiction to what they were saying and relating this way of thinking to my own upbringing, I felt the lights come on. Once I completed the program and became a certified sex addiction therapist (CSAT), I set off to center my treatment modality on this substantial neuroscientific research, intensifying the link between developmental trauma and sex addiction. To further enhance my research, I began training in somatic experiencing (SE), eye movement desensitization and reprocessing (EMDR), brainspotting, sensorimotor psychotherapy, and the psychological approach to couples therapy (PACT). Thus, TINSA was born, an unprecedented model that applies neurobiology specifically to sex addiction to support research on how to best treat the core issues that are the undeniable catalyst for sex addiction.

This book is neither sex negative nor moralistic. On the contrary, the information provided within these pages emphatically promotes healthy, enriching sex and aims to equip addicts with the ability to thrive within healthy, sex-filled, meaningful relationships. Recovery from sex addiction is not about morals. It's about helping people who are deeply hurt, and who are deeply hurting others, to find freedom from their imprisoning behaviors. It is my hope that any person suffering from sex addiction can begin the healing process, seek additional treatment, and live a life enriched with healthy sex and meaningful relationships.

MB

Acknowledgments

I would like to acknowledge the men I have worked with over the past ten years who have demonstrated unparalleled courage to face and be rid of the lifelong patterns of self-regulation. Born out of their earliest experiences, addiction left them with only one option: to forego the joy of actual connection out of the need to protect their own emotional, mental, and physical safety. The men I have had the privilege to work with have faced public ridicule, misunderstanding, and vilification, and have had to deal with the wrath and destruction created while caught in the personal hell of sex and pornography addictions.

This book could also not be possible if not for the work of the pioneers who forged a new understanding of an age-old problem—sexual addiction. My special thanks go to Dr. Patrick Carnes, who taught me that this problem is real and treatable. I am grateful to him for facing the early and ongoing onslaught of naysayers who insisted that this very real addiction is but an excuse with no valid research to prove its existence. Dr. Carnes singlehandedly brought light to a condition that affects millions, and because of his courageous and unwavering study and exploration, he will go down as one of the great innovators in the fields of addiction and psychology.

I cannot fully express the deep gratitude I hold for the innovators and courageous people involved in neurobiology, trauma, and addictions. Their influential work allowed me to develop a model for the treatment of sexual addiction by allowing me to help clients with a deeper understanding of how their adverse experiences actually affected their nervous systems, thus predisposing them to addictive behavior. These men and women have drastically changed my worldview on addiction, in both my personal and my professional life. Their preeminent works helped me to more deeply understand how our autonomic nervous system has a much deeper role that, when understood, can help us live more free and conscious lives.

I would like to acknowledge David Grand, Francine Shapiro, Peter Levine, Pat Ogden, and Marsha Linehan for giving me the tools and the protocols to actually treat the core of addictive behaviors. These tools have forever changed the way sex addiction can be treated; they allow remission while also freeing the sufferer from lifelong patterns of unconscious and ineffective need gratification, enabling one to finally find authenticity, vulnerability, and wholehearted intimacy.

I would not be here myself if it were not for the organizations Alcoholics Anonymous and Sex Addicts Anonymous, which welcomed me and showed me truth, regardless of how deeply I believed I was flawed, unworthy, shameful, and did not belong. Without these organizations I would not have been able to maintain any semblance of sobriety, nor would I have found that recovery is possible.

I would also like to thank my editor, Marianne Harkin, who, no matter how many questions I asked or how neurotic I became, both assured me that I was able to complete this important work and magically formulated my concepts into readable and understandable information.

To my family, thank you for your continued support and unconditional love.

One

What Sex Addiction Is Really Like

If you're reading this book, you or someone you know may be suffering from what is known as sexual addiction. Perhaps you have experienced negative consequences in your marriage, your relationships, your job, your social reputation, your self-esteem, your health, your finances, your daily routines, and your overall happiness, that are directly related to your compulsive sexual behaviors. You may feel as if you have no control over your life and that you are totally dictated by your compulsion to act out sexually. You may often ask yourself questions such as "Why me?" "Why can't I control myself?" and "What's wrong with me?"

On the other hand, you may actually bristle at the idea that somehow, some way, you have lost control over your sexual behaviors. You may tell yourself that all men do it or that it's just a "guy thing." You may have heard of the term *sex addiction*, but because of the negative stigma attached, you have steered clear of owning your own addiction and the negative impact that it has had on yourself and others. The denial of sex addiction may be perpetuated by the fear that you will be labeled. In hearing the term *sex addict*, you may well have conjured up images of sex offenders and social pariahs, and you know that you're not one of *those people*. But despite the incredible effort you put forth to keep yourself in denial, the deep-seated shame that you feel regarding your chronic sexual behavior has left you feeling awful. You likely fear that at any given moment you will be discovered for the person you believe you truly are—someone unworthy of affection and connection.

Likewise, if you are reading this and you are the partner of a person whose sexual behaviors have spiraled out of control, your feelings and emotions may also be all over the map. You may think that your spouse or partner is some kind of sociopath, unable to feel any empathy or have any regard for fidelity or vows of commitment. As for this term *sex addiction*, you may also have your doubts, dismissing it as merely an excuse that men can use in order to carry on a life of lies and cheating.

As a sex addiction therapist for over ten years, I have been faced with all kinds of rebuttals and counterarguments that challenge the legitimacy of this addiction. In my practice, I have even been told that I am "sex negative" and "puritanical" and that people have a human right to express their sexuality. These arguments remind me of the ones I used while still active in my own sex addiction and alcoholism, defending my own unhealthy behaviors.

Adding fuel to the fire are others who claim that sex addiction is a scam and that there is no science to confirm that this addiction even exists. These naysayers accuse sex addiction proponents of creating a fictitious disease in order to make a profit. However, a large body of empirical evidence exists in the area of addiction and specifically sex addiction that will, hopefully, silence these pundits and end the hold they have over any person who seeks recovery.

Whatever emotions, thoughts, or doubts you may be experiencing, if you are reading this book, you or someone very close to you has been engaging in sexual behavior that is causing everyone involved an incredible amount of pain. If you are a person whose sexual behaviors have left you at risk of losing your marriage, family, children, reputation, and job, you may be reading this book because you are desperate but unable to change these behaviors, and maybe you are willing to look at this problem with your sexuality as an addiction. Be assured there is great relief when a secret life finally makes it to the light of day. When you are able to own your addiction, you no longer have to hide. Owning your addiction means that you no longer need to keep up your double life. Most importantly, once you are able to own your sex addiction, there is a real opportunity to heal yourself and your relationships.

So how, exactly, is sex addiction defined? The term itself was coined by psychologist Patrick Carnes in his groundbreaking book *Out of the Shadows: Understanding Sexual Addiction* (2001). Carnes defines sex addiction as "any sexually related, compulsive behavior which interferes with normal living and causes severe stress on family, friends, loved ones and one's work environment." As sex addiction therapist Robert Weiss (2015a.) puts it, sexual addiction is "a dysfunctional preoccupation with sexual fantasy and behavior, often involving the obsessive pursuit of non-intimate sex, pornography, compulsive masturbation, romantic intensity, and objectified partner sex." Weiss (2015a.) continues this definition to assert that this adult obsessive pattern of thoughts and behaviors continues for a period of at least six months despite the following:

- attempts made to self-correct the problematic sexual behavior
- promises made to self and others to change the sexual behavior
- significant, directly related negative life consequences

What these professionals are saying is that there is a difference between someone who is in control of his sexual behaviors and someone who is not, and that difference is addiction. When someone is addicted to sex, he cannot stop the behavior, even if he wants to and even if he experiences negative life consequences as a direct result. A sex addict is at risk for sexually transmitted diseases, financial ruin, legal troubles, shattered personal relationships, loss of reputation or career, and an ever-deepening self-loathing and mistrust.

Of course, we've all seen these negative consequences and downfalls play out on television and in the lives of multiple celebrities and high-profile figures who could not control their sexual behaviors. In these instances where public figures were outed for their promiscuity, they suffered major detrimental consequences as a direct result. A golf legend lost his wife and endured public embarrassment for years to come. A former US president was not only publicly embarrassed for his chronic sexual activities but was also impeached for perjury and obstruction of justice because he lied under oath about his affair. A New York congressman lost his chance at becoming New York City's mayor simply because he could not refrain from sexting women on social media; he also ultimately lost his wife and has to endure jail time. And then of course there is the TV and movie actor who is well known for his philandering reputation that led to his multiple divorces and who has recently come forward as HIV positive.

Why would such powerful men, who seemingly have everything, risk marriages, careers, health, and reputations, all for simple sexual gratification? Only when you actually start to peel back the layers of this issue can you really begin to grasp that for some people who act out sexually, their behaviors are uncontrollable. Despite negative life consequences, these individuals continued to act out simply because *they could not stop.*

The scope and magnitude of this problem goes far beyond Hollywood and politics. In my practice, I have had a client who lost his job with a Fortune 500 company because he could not stop looking at pornography when he was at work. In spite of the multiple forewarnings that he was going to lose everything he had ever worked for, he continued the behavior and was fired because the compulsion to log on every afternoon at three fifteen was too strong to resist.

It is estimated that between 3 and 5 percent of the US population (roughly nine million people) struggle with uncontrollable chronic sexual behaviors. As if those statistics are not shocking enough, they are undoubtedly low simply because the untreated and unreported population are not among these numbers. To really grasp the gravity of this issue, one must be willing to acknowledge the many other red flags warning us that sex and pornography addiction is an escalating crisis within our society. Lee Chris reported that as of 2011, nearly forty million Americans log on to one or more of the 4.2 million pornographic websites in existence each day (Newsweek.com, November 25, 2011). Also, in 2016 pornography was deemed an epidemic by Utah state legislation, stating that it is a "health hazard" that promotes "the objectification of women, which teaches girls they are to be used and teaches boys to be users" (Domonoske 2016). If you carefully consider such facts as these, it is easy to see that addiction to sex and pornography is not only real but it is a national crisis snowballing out of control.

Well-substantiated evidence exists that suggests sex addiction is not that different from substance addiction. In 2010, The American Society of Addiction Medicine (ASAM), a psychotherapeutic professional organization that has fully accepted sex as an addiction, made a departure from equating addiction solely with substance dependence by redefining addiction altogether. In a public statement released the same year, ASAM defined all addiction in terms of brain changes, stating that addiction is a primary, chronic disease of brain reward, motivation, memory and related circuitry. Dysfunction in these circuits leads to characteristic biological, psychological, social and spiritual manifestations. This is reflected in an individual pathologically pursuing reward and relief by substance use and other behaviors. Addiction is characterized as an inability to consistently abstain, impairment in behavioral control, cravings, diminished recognition of significant problems with one's behaviors and interpersonal relationships, and a dysfunctional emotional response. Like other chronic diseases, addiction often involves cycles of relapse and remission. Without treatment or engagement in recovery activities, addiction is progressive and can result in disability or premature death. (ASAM 2017)

The fact that the term *sexual addiction* is not listed in the fifth edition of the *Diagnostic & Statistical Manual* ([*DSM-5*] 2013) is one of the strongest arguments that counters this way of thinking. The *DSM-5*'s publisher, the American Psychiatric Association (APA), does not recognize the term *sex addiction*, stating that it is too broad. The APA *does*, however, recognize the terms *hypersexuality* and *hyper sexual behavior*. What is most important to recognize here is that the APA is not overly accepting of behavioral addictions in general, and in fact has refrained from using the term *addiction* whatsoever. They even go so far as to label alcoholism and drug addiction instead as "substance *disorders*," with diagnostic criteria set in place for such disorders.

For alcohol use disorder, the APA lists in their *DSM-5* the following diagnostic criteria, each of which is in synchronicity with sex addiction:

1. Alcohol is often taken in larger amounts or over a longer period than was intended.
2. There is a persistent desire or unsuccessful efforts to cut down or control alcohol use.
3. A great deal of time is spent in activities necessary to obtain alcohol, use alcohol, or recover from its effects.
4. Craving, or a strong desire or urge, to use alcohol.
5. Recurrent alcohol use resulting in a failure to fulfill major role obligations at work, school, or home.
6. Continued alcohol use despite having persistent or recurrent social or interpersonal problems caused or exacerbated by the effects of alcohol.

7. Important social, occupational, or recreational activities are given up or reduced because of alcohol use.
8. Recurrent alcohol use in situations in which it is physically hazardous.
9. Alcohol use is continued despite knowledge of having a persistent or recurrent physical or psychological problem that is likely to have been caused or exacerbated by alcohol.
10. Tolerance, as defined by either of the following: a) A need for markedly increased amounts of alcohol to achieve intoxication or desired effect b) A markedly diminished effect with continued use of the same amount of alcohol.
11. Withdrawal, as manifested by either of the following: a) The characteristic withdrawal syndrome for alcohol (refer to criteria A and B of the criteria set for alcohol withdrawal) b) Alcohol (or a closely related substance, such as a benzodiazepine) is taken to relieve or avoid withdrawal symptoms. (2013, 490)

As with each of these criteria where alcohol is the vice and the overwhelming cause of a person's own demise despite best efforts to stop, sex can and is being used by millions of people in the exact same way. ASAM, too, has its own diagnostic criteria that apply to all addictions. The three main criteria on this list are the same criteria I apply in my practice to sex addiction and are as follows:

- preoccupation or obsession with substance or behavior
- loss of control evidenced by failed attempts to quit or cut back
- inability to stop despite directly related negative consequences

In all of these ways, sex addiction is just like any other addiction. Sex addiction does not equal sex offending, perversion, homosexuality, or transgenderism. It is a craving, preoccupation, compulsion, and inability to stop engaging in the behavior despite negative consequences.

Mention sex addiction to someone with no experience with the disease, and they are likely to joke about it as if it were a lighthearted or even desirable condition. Unfortunately, the reality of sex addiction is painful. It is a life of constant duplicity, paranoia, shame, fear, anxiety, depression, isolation, and loneliness, coupled with self-inflicted jolts of adrenaline and dissociation. The addict often feels different from everyone else, trapped in a dark, secret life of obsession and constraint. While they are deeply ashamed of their behaviors, it is usually the lying, secrecy, and lack of personal integrity that cause the most pain. Patrick Carnes stated that one of the four core beliefs of the sex addict is, "No one would love me as I am" (2001, 173).

In order to begin your journey to recovery, you must first fully recognize and accept that you are indeed addicted. So how does one know if he is a sex or pornography addict? Let's look at the common characteristics of a sex addict so that you can correctly assess if you fall into this category. If you do find that your compulsive behaviors align with these common characteristics, then you will find the information provided here to be profoundly life altering. Equipped with the knowledge of the underlying causes of this addiction, any persons suffering will begin to be able to regain control over their compulsive behaviors and take back their life.

In my ten years of treating only sex and pornography addictions, I have empirically validated the common traits of people suffering from sex and porn addiction. Those traits are as follows:

- inability to be authentic (resulting in being fake or putting on an act)
- inability to be vulnerable
- inability to respond with empathy
- lack of parental attunement
- deeply damaged sense of self
- inability to fully connect
- avoidant attachment personality type (self-regulation)
- raised in environments that did not support emotions or autonomy
- inability to regulate emotional states in normal, healthy ways
- re-creation/repetition and unsuccessful attempts to heal developmental wounds
- inability to bond
- inability to maintain meaningful relationships

Other characteristics may include narcissistic tendencies, preying on vulnerability, very low self-esteem or damaged belief system, deceitfulness, lying, denial, defensiveness, guilt, shame, and manipulation.

Aside from those listed above, other additional commonalities could also be indicators of addiction. In many cases, the sex addict harbors internal beliefs about not fitting in or ever being loved. Sex addicts feel that they have never been in a relationship in which their significant other knew who they really were. Their partners often say that they are not present or mindful. Addicts may perpetually feel abandoned, unwanted, scared, helpless, hurt, lonely, and isolated, and they use sex outside of the primary relationship to keep these feelings at bay. This way, they believe that they can receive the benefits of intimacy without having to be authentically vulnerable or intimate.

Throughout my practice, I have also seen another commonality across the board. Each of my clients, as well as each individual that I have ever met who suffers from sex addiction, consistently reports a personal history of adverse developmental experiences. Either they did not receive correct attunement as a child, were not validated for who they were, or were raised in an emotional vacuum. There is much research identifying such experiences as a catalyst for addiction. When childhood wounding occurs, a person's brain and nervous system may respond differently from those who did not experience developmental traumas. From an early age, these individuals can begin to seek outside behaviors and substances to regulate these damaged anatomic systems. Because sexual activity is one of the first pleasure-producing behaviors we find, it is no wonder that many people in these circumstances begin to use sexual behavior as a regulation tool. When continued into adulthood, however, these chronic, compulsive, and unhealthy sexual behaviors manifest as what they truly are: symptoms of a much deeper issue. Neuroscientist and addiction specialist Gabor Maté states that he never asks why the addiction, but instead asks, why the pain? The progressive treatment modality presented in this book not only offers insight into the why but also provides a solid methodology to heal the root causes of this disease.

The addict engages in behaviors that are destructive to self and others. One client of mine reported that despite knowing that the company he worked for was tracking his cell phone use, he continued to call 900 numbers anyway and was fired. I have seen multiple cases in which men promised their partners and themselves to stop, only to be rediscovered repeating the same behaviors within months. In all of the cases that I have witnessed firsthand, these people continued engaging in unhealthy sexual behaviors even at the likely expense of their careers, reputations, and families. To the average person, these behaviors might seem insane, but a clinician treating pornography and sexual addiction hears stories like these every day.

What could possibly drive seemingly lunatic behavior like this? Answering this question is the key component to complete and long-term healing. In my ten years of treating this addiction, I have found my clients to have an absolute inability to regulate or express their emotions without participating in a behavior that changes their neurological chemistry. These individuals use sexual behaviors primarily as a way in which to discharge emotion, increase emotion, or re-create unresolved adverse developmental experiences (ADEs). My experience in sexual addiction therapy, combined with careful study of the neuroscientific research regarding addiction, has led me to conclude that the brain and nervous system can be predisposed to this way of operation, utilizing addictive behaviors such as sexual pleasure to relieve emotional dysregulation.

Addiction is a solution that absolutely works, at least initially. Addiction is a guaranteed solution that has the capacity to make everything better. Long term, however, this "solution" is as helpful and sustainable as a small bandage on a very deep cut. While addiction does its job at killing pain and helping people temporarily cope, this treatment comes with a long list of side effects. Unfortunately for those of us who have partaken in this "guaranteed solution," it seems that we missed the fine print: This substance or behavior will act as a solution to all of your problems; however, using this solution will cost you your happiness, your ability to connect, and your dignity. Continued use will cost you your relationships, family, career, reputation, self-fulfillment, and very possibly your life.

The problem with partaking in chronic sexual behaviors as a way to mend old wounds is that you will feel good (or at least not as bad) for a while, but nothing changes. You will return to the very same place you always have been, a place where you are incapable of sustaining intimate connections and personal happiness.

When sexual behaviors escalate to the point of being used compulsively, this is a sign of deeper issues. At the core of sex addiction is the inability to form a truly intimate bond with a significant other. For sex addicts, the deeper issues that inhibit this bonding began to form early on in our development. Truly intimate bonding requires a capacity for vulnerability, a quality that sex addicts lack due to adverse developmental experiences. These adverse experiences affect the brain and nervous systems in such a way that these systems begin to see and read vulnerability and intimacy as threatening.

The following is an important equation that you will hear multiple times throughout the following chapters:

Vulnerability + Authenticity = Intimacy

Although the addict avoids vulnerability and authenticity like the plague, it is this very avoidance that perpetuates the need to act out. Of course, there are very good reasons to avoid these ways of being, as these basic building blocks of intimacy were typically abused, threatened, or destroyed in adverse developmental experiences.

Just as alcohol or drug use is an attempt to kill or modulate pain, when relied upon over a sustained amount of time, sex can also change our anatomy to the point where we become reliant on the chemicals that are produced through the behavior. So while we may *begin* using sexual behavior simply to feel good in an otherwise oppressed natural environment, we might *continue* engaging in the behavior because our anatomy becomes dependent on it. Of course, not all people who engage in sexual activity become addicts, just as not all people become addicts to even very addictive substances like heroin; but for some people, sexual behavior used in this way can certainly become an addiction.

Until recently, the addiction community relied heavily on a genetic explanation for the predisposition of addiction. However, thanks to the proliferation of brain research, the addiction community is shying away from that explanation and shifting more toward environmental reasons. These new findings demonstrate that genes do still matter; however, our environment (especially our early environment) is a more likely catalyst for addiction than a supposed "addiction gene." In 2010, Gabor Maté demonstrated that an addiction gene does not exist, and that while genes can influence such things as temperament and our level of sensitivity, they cannot and do not influence even simple behaviors. For example, our ancestors may have given us our blue eyes and a propensity for being quick to anger, but it is the way we were raised that influences what we do with that anger. Maté (2010) showed that our behaviors are determined by how our environmental factors influence our genes, and not how our genes influence our environment. Thus, the adverse developmental experiences that occurred when we were very young, completely helpless, and vulnerable are the beginnings to our addictive lifestyle.

Addiction of any kind is a full-time endeavor, and sex and pornography addictions are no different. It is a constant effort to stay emotionally regulated, followed by a constant attempt to avoid the pain of withdrawal. However, there is hope. Treatment for this crippling disease is entering a new frontier. It is becoming apparent that we need to address the damages done to the autonomic and neurological systems in order to achieve recovery, and unless we do so, behavioral approaches will continue to struggle.

Two

Trauma and Its Role in Addiction

Trauma is subjective. Not everyone who experiences a traumatic event or events will be affected in the same way. It is up to each individual whether an event is personally traumatic. So, what exactly is trauma, and how does it relate to sex addiction? In order to fully understand and treat sex addiction, we must first gain some rudimentary knowledge of what trauma is and the impact it can have on a person.

TINSA defines trauma as any experience that overwhelms our ability to process incoming information both at the time of the experience and in future situations. Many experts believe trauma occurs when our natural defenses are unable to protect us from physical, mental, or emotional harm.

Trauma comes in many forms. It can include

- sexual assault or abuse
- physical assault or abuse
- emotional or psychological trauma
- serious accidents, illnesses, or medical procedures
- natural or manmade disaster
- witnessing violence, including domestic abuse
- school violence, including bullying
- traumatic grief or separation
- war or terrorism
- betrayal or relational trauma

Many experts divide traumatic events into two categories: *big*-T *traumas* and *little*-t *traumas*. While big-*T* traumas are generally associated with a single catastrophic event, little-*t* traumas are less noticeable but are just as damaging to a person's psyche. Although trauma is usually equated with life-altering events, such as the devastation of the World Trade Center on September 11, 2001, or the impact of Hurricane Katrina on New Orleans, the truth is that traumatized individuals can often trace their adverse developmental experiences back to events that one might think of as inconsequential. Trauma insulates us from the world around us without our being fully aware of that loss of connection.

In my experience with treating addiction, I have found that most often my clients have been subjected to traumatic experiences that most experts would consider to be little-*t* traumas. These include any events or experiences that affected their brains and nervous systems over time through a series of ongoing behaviors. If they occur during the early developmental stages of life, little-*t* traumas have the capability to impact how children view themselves, their relationships, and their place in the world. The long-term effects of little-*t* traumas result in a person growing up with a fear of abandonment, a feeling of not belonging, or with a constant need to be on guard against possible invasion or pain. That person will also suffer from an inability to form true intimate relationships.

Human beings are instinctual creatures, but instinct can be skewed by trauma; traumatic events can prevent us from being able to access appropriate responses, especially if they occur early on in life. When we are subjected to traumatic and overwhelming situations, especially from a young age, our instinctual responses can be obstructed. We become traumatized when our ability to respond to a perceived threat is in some way overwhelmed. This inability to adequately respond can impact us in obvious ways as well as subtle ones, such as hyperarousal, panic, rage, rigidness, obsessions, or chronic anxiety. Alternatively, we can experience feelings of powerlessness, helplessness, shame, or immobility.

Although both big-*T* traumas and little-*t* traumas can lead to addiction, it is the little-*t* traumas that are most commonly reported. Ongoing psychological or emotional trauma in the form of terrifying and overwhelming experiences during their early childhood is most often disclosed. The first step to healing is to recognize any events that you may have experienced where people hurt you physically, mentally, emotionally, or spiritually, either intentionally or unintentionally. To identify the root cause of your addiction, you must pinpoint where in your life you reached out to connect, only to be left with the inability to have that connection completed. The following are examples of traumatic occurrences commonly reported by those who suffer from sex addiction:

- They were not attuned to by their caregiver.
- They were invalidated for who they were.
- They were not emotionally recognized.

- They were either told or were otherwise made to believe that they were not good enough for their parents or peers.
- They felt rejected or abandoned.
- They were subjected to parental divorce or death of a loved one.
- They experienced a loss of a pet, friendship, or young love.
- They may have been terrified of or controlled by another's anger.
- They were not permitted to pursue their desires or interests.
- They were made to feel bad or insignificant because others were distant, cold, or punishing.
- They were punished, rejected, or ridiculed for being authentic (being themselves).
- They were made to feel stupid or inadequate about their intelligence.
- They were dismissed, minimized, ignored, disregarded, shamed, or ridiculed for their feelings, thoughts, physical appearance, or spiritual beliefs.
- They were made responsible for regulating others' emotions (e.g., Mom or Dad's confidence).
- They were made responsible for making the family look good.
- They were punched, hit, kicked, slapped, or violently shaken.
- They were sexually abused.
- They were made to feel unsafe or threatened with exclusion and alienation.
- They were forced to avoid having feelings.
- They were not properly instructed on how to connect with, understand, and resolve their emotions.

What is important to note here is that most people experience many of the above occurrences at one time or another. The difference between most addicts and people who do not become addicts is that nonaddicted people are able to resolve the effects of these occurrences, but addicts cannot, and it is these unresolved issues that lead to addiction.

After hearing hundreds of similar accounts where early childhood traumas or ADEs were consistently reported by my clients, I quickly began to understand that these experiences were directly related to their sexual addictions. I saw that while the sexual behaviors were often different, the core of their addictions was surprising similar. The most common forms of adverse developmental experiences reported among sufferers of sexual addiction are a lack of attunement and protection, thwarted emotional development, invalidation, and abandonment. These deficiencies are not about bad parenting, but about a parent's inability to respond to the child's emotional needs. Most parents are doing the best they can with the tools they have, but whether deliberately or inadvertently, the traumas of our childhood can have tremendous impact on our lives. The following sections provide detailed descriptions of the damaging impacts that each of these traumas can have.

Lack of Attunement

Psychologists and therapists have long known the importance of attachment and attunement when it comes to human health and relationships. However, most clients do not have an understanding of this vital developmental process. When asked if they received proper attunement as a child, most of my clients answer yes and report an above-normal amount of physical care. They proudly report that they come from homes where there was plenty of food, clean water, heat, and adequate clothing. But none of this has much to do with the process of parental attunement, and so it is very clear that this process is widely misunderstood.

"The attachment figure is intended to be the source of joy, connection, and emotional soothing," according to Daniel Siegel (2017). "Instead, the experience of the child who develops a disorganized attachment is such that the caregiver is actually the source of alarm, fear, and terror, so the child cannot turn to the attachment figure to be soothed." Because attachment is linked to attunement and being adequately cared for as a child, attachment without attunement is not enough for optimal development. Proper development and the process of attunement have very little to do with having the right clothes, enough food, or adequate shelter. Instead, attunement is the ability of a caregiver to adequately and consistently respond to the child's nonverbal cues for attention and regulation. It means that our nonverbal responses and distress cues are met appropriately. It is something that occurs between a caregiver and a child that has to be consistent and positive and constant.

An example of a scenario when attunement is not met is when a parental figure leaves his or her child in another room during a time of distress hoping that the child will "cry it out." There are also less extreme and more subtle ways in which attunement is not met. While Mom and Dad may have held you when you were crying, she or he may not have been able to be more deeply attuned to you and soothe you when you were in distress and when you couldn't communicate what you needed. We have all seen the nervous parent holding a crying baby, walking back and forth and bouncing the baby as if that will stop it from crying. That is the lack of attunement. As you are well aware, outside of crying and screaming, for about the first year and a half of their lives, children cannot verbally communicate their needs. Therefore, in order to properly attend to his or her child, a parent must connect in other ways. This can be done through skin-to-skin touch, eye-to-eye communication, or simply by being present and connected to his or her offspring. Psychologists state that it is this intimate contact that is essential for healthy brain development. In other words, attunement is necessary in order for our neurological systems to engage and function properly. When the caregiver is responding to the child's nonverbal cues adequately through eye-to-eye and skin-to-skin contact, what he or she is actually doing is attuning to and regulating the child's nervous system.

Although one might assume that attunement and the use of nonverbal forms of communication with their child should come naturally to parents, for some it does not. Attunement and the ability to express intimacy with another human being is a learned skill that is passed down from generation to generation. It is not a genetic inheritance but is something that is either environmentally present or absent.

Attunement is a skill set and ability that is ideally observed, experienced, absorbed, and acquired by a child through the actions and care of the parent. However, a child who does not receive proper attunement will grow up unable to attune to his or her own offspring. This does not point to faulty or bad parenting, but instead demonstrates that you cannot give what you do not possess. If our parents or our caregivers did not receive adequate attunement, then they themselves will not be able to respond appropriately to their own children's nonverbal cues. Of course this does not make someone a bad parent, as they are merely wired and configured to respond to their own children in the same way that they were responded to as children. In addition to this, there are many other reasons that a parent may not be able to attune to his or her child. Perhaps a parent must go to work to provide for the family and is overwhelmed and preoccupied in other areas of life. Maybe a parent simply has too many children to be able to properly and sufficiently attune to each one. Additionally, if a caregiver suffers from any kind of intimacy or attachment disorder or has an addiction or mental health problem, that may also prevent him or her from being able to give the emotional and neurological regulation that the child needs. Whatever the case may be, if a parent cannot provide what is needed for a child's system to fully develop, the child may be left with no other option than to begin searching for his or her own way to regulate and express emotions. And this is the breeding ground upon which addiction can begin.

A lack of attunement might be the single most important variable in the predisposition to addictive behavior. To the infant the world is a mirror, and if that mirror is not reflecting back what the child needs, he or she will not develop an internal locus of control. For a healthy brain and nervous system to develop, the infant requires the help of the caregiver's stronger and more regulated nervous system. Much like scaffolding surrounds a building under construction, the infant's ability to access, understand, regulate, and appropriately express emotions must be brought online through the parent's ability to access these same attributes. If a mother or father has a healthy, functioning nervous system, chances are that she or he will be able to provide comforting neurological regulation. However, if a parent or caregiver, for whatever reason, lacks the ability to scaffold the child's emotional development and regulate the child's nervous system, the child will be handicapped in these vital areas that are required for future healthy bonding.

I have seen very few sexually addicted clients who had their nonverbal cues responded to appropriately as children. At a time when they were most vulnerable, they experienced hurt and neglect as their authentic self and authentic expression was hindered or not allowed. When proper attunement does not happen, it is read by the brain as a threat to survival, and a small child, having no other ability to respond, will be forced into immobility. The child, with no other means of getting his or her needs met, has to choose between attunement (getting needs met) and survival.

Thwarted Emotional Development

In Patrick Carnes's (1992) landmark study, 87 percent of sex addicts reported coming from families that were disengaged, detached, uninvolved, and emotionally absent. The people I treat live in a world devoid of true emotional experience and expression. Feelings are problematic and seen as a liability or are so uncomfortable that they need to be avoided. Unfortunately, there can be no connection or intimacy without the authentic and vulnerable expression of emotions. My clients have a very difficult time identifying their emotions, or if they can identify what they feel, they then often lack the skills required to regulate or express these emotions. Addicts either tend to avoid, suppress, deny, or ignore emotions, or they overly express emotions without an ability to regulate themselves. Just as with attunement, these characteristics regarding emotion are learned, not innate. They are passed down generationally through early environmental observations, experiences, and conditions within our households or other early surroundings that fine-tuned the systems we use for emotional expression.

When discussing how emotions were treated within their formative years, many of my clients report that emotions simply were either not allowed or deeply discouraged. Furthermore, when asked how common emotions such as fear, sadness, anger, or joy were handled in their families, many of my clients either can't recall, or they remember being told to "grow up," "quit being a baby," or "get over it." In some cases, my clients report that emotional expression was met with a stronger emotional response by the parent, such as hitting, punishing, or ridicule. In other words, they reported that during their development, emotional expression was severely avoided or immediately stifled.

The outcome of being raised in emotionally vacant or emotionally abusive environments such as these is that the child learns that his or her emotions are invalid or that any emotion expressed is bad, wrong, and certainly dangerous. At the core, my clients repeatedly show that their emotional states were never seen as having value. This too can set a person up for addiction. When people are never given the opportunity to express emotion, they also never learn how to regulate their emotions, so they are led down a rabbit hole of constantly seeking other ways by which to regulate their emotions, either through behaviors or substances.

Lack of Protection

Just as important as proper attunement and the need and ability to complete our connection response is our need for adequate protection. Like attunement, protection is much more than the physical safety that is afforded to us through food and shelter. Protection comes from valuing the child's individual needs for safety, including physical, emotional, mental, and spiritual safety. In order to be adequately protected, an individual's physical and emotional vulnerabilities, as well as the ability and encouragement of authentic expression, must be safeguarded. Additionally, if one parent fails to protect the child from the lack of attunement by the other parent, that is also a lack of protection. For example, a baby recently put to bed for the night starts crying. Mom goes to pick her up, but Dad says, "No, you'll only spoil her. Let her cry." That is lack of protection.

Of course, very young children cannot adequately protect themselves physically or emotionally from much of anything. What this does is lead to lesser survival and defense mechanisms such as immobilization or fight-or-flight responses. While we will be discussing these responses in depth in future chapters, it is important to understand that a lack of protection can be traumatizing and cause seriously debilitating effects on a person's neurological functioning.

With respect to protection, not only have my clients reported being neglected or refused emotional support during times of physical or emotional danger as children, but in some cases they have reported being invalidated, disbelieved, or even punished when they reached out for help. The repercussions that a lack of protection can have on a child are immense. When a child's physical and emotional vulnerabilities are not protected, his or her instinctual responses can become obstructed, forcing the child to rely on him- or herself for protection and predisposing the child to seek behaviors and substances to aid in emotional regulation.

Invalidation

To validate means to find value in something or someone. A sense of validation for our authentic worth is absolutely required for healthy emotional development. Parents and caregivers often neglect to value their children's individual worth and instead attempt to make their children "better" by setting unattainable or unreasonable standards. This is driven by the often-shallow society in which we live, which demonstrates a value of accomplishments and material possessions over a person's basic emotional components. When love is only given by a parent to a child for an accomplishment, it negates the positive effects of love because it teaches the child that he or she is valuable for what he or she does, not who he or she is. When a person's authentic self is not valued from a very young age, this creates a large void, which that person is then constantly looking to fill. My clients all suffer from deep wounds of invalidation, and most of them are attempting to make up for this by finding validation in their sexual conquests.

Abandonment

Many of my clients are shocked at the idea that they experienced abandonment in their early environments. They report that their parents were *always* present and *never* left them on their own. Although it is true that some people do experience childhood abandonment in the most literal sense of the word— by being left unattended, usually either through divorce or a parent's death— the term *abandonment* as it is used in relation to addiction is more understood to be a consistent pattern of the caregiver's inability to be emotionally present for the child's needs. Again, this is not about bad parenting, but rather about the parent's inability to adequately respond to the child's verbal or nonverbal requests for connection and protection. Addicts live in terror of being left or excluded. These feelings derive from abandonment wounds and having their needs unintentionally unattended or unresolved.

As you may have noticed, these five adverse developmental experiences that are most frequently reported by sufferers of sex addiction share a single commonality: they all relate to how the family unit handled emotional protection and bonding when the child was developing his or her vulnerability and authenticity. In short, TINSA defines trauma as the result of being injured while vulnerable or when being authentic.

Vulnerability plus authenticity enables intimacy. Since sex addiction is defined as an intimacy disorder, it is not surprising then that the two most common characteristics contributing to the formation and progression of sex addiction are wounds to an individual's innate vulnerability and expression of authenticity, both of which can threaten a person's capacity to be intimate. Although these wounds most frequently occur within the family unit and within the first years of a person's life, they can also occur outside of the family unit and at any time throughout a person's developmental lifespan.

Wounds to Vulnerability

A vulnerable state of being is one in which a person is open, unguarded, unsuspecting, defenseless, innocent, or without the ability to protect oneself or regulate one's emotions. Because small children are vulnerable by nature (without the capacity to care for or defend themselves), they are especially susceptible to being emotionally wounded. The word *vulnerable* is derived from the Latin word *vulnus*, meaning "wound." While at one time, vulnerability meant being exposed to the possibility of a physical wound, in modern times when we speak of vulnerability, we define it as being defenseless or open to the possibility of being wounded in a nonphysical or emotional manner. It means that you are without defense and that you are susceptible to being wounded, criticized, or attacked.

Vulnerability, as described above, allows us to connect with others. Used against us, however, it can be terribly damaging to our emotional state. Most of our formative years are composed of a complete reliance on stronger individuals just for basic survival. While we are all born vulnerable and unable to defend ourselves or meet our own needs, wounds to our vulnerability that occur during our formative years can have a serious negative impact on our ability to be vulnerable later on in life. These wounds can have profound effects on our brain, the functioning of our autonomic nervous system, our personal beliefs, and our ability to form trusting connections with others. In short, wounds to a person's vulnerability can both hinder his or her ability to be vulnerable and cause that person to purposely avoid vulnerability with others. This can set a person up for addiction. Listed here are some of the ways in which a person can be wounded when vulnerable:

- being unable to process emotional, physical, and sexual experiences that were overwhelming
- being controlled emotionally through anger or ridicule
- being told how to feel or what to feel
- reaching out to connect but being unable to receive connection
- being hurt physically, mentally, emotionally, or spiritually, whether intentionally or unintentionally
- experiencing events such as divorce, death, loss of a pet, friendship, or young love
- experiencing events that made you feel scared, hurt, shamed, embarrassed, confused, helpless, and abandoned
- being rejected or made to feel inferior or inadequate
- being teased, bullied, or harassed
- getting punched, hit, kicked, slapped, or violently shaken
- being made to feel unsafe or threatened with exclusion and alienation
- being used by others to make themselves feel better
- being made responsible for making the family look good
- being forced to avoid or suppress feelings

- not properly being instructed about how to connect with, understand, and resolve your emotions
- not being taught simple skills like reading, writing, how to play sports, or other basic activities
- growing up in an environment where emotional expression was not allowed
- growing up in an environment where nonverbal needs were not met and verbal expressions were ignored
- being adversely affected by caregivers who were unable to handle pain or emotion themselves
- being shamed for your emotions or your body
- being raised in an environment where you were not allowed to be who you are
- being emotionally neglected and emotionally abused
- being physically or sexually assaulted

Being vulnerable means we can allow ourselves to remain open, even at the possibility of getting hurt. But sometimes when a person is consistently exposed to adverse developmental experiences like the ones just listed, they begin to close themselves off. When this happens to a person from a very early age, he or she begins missing out on important neurological and socially developmental milestones. Due to fear of getting hurt or rejected, children who have had adverse experiences may decide not to take as many risks in their social circles or in their academics as other children their age. As a result, their emotional growth will become stunted.

What I experienced in my upbringing was a mother who was rather abusive to me from a very early age. My parents were both much older at the time that I was born, and I was not exactly a welcome surprise. Although I can certainly remember episodes of personal neglect and abuse that occurred from the time I was four years old, I have been told that my mother was actually physically rough and reckless with me from when I was about six months old. In addition to this, I don't think the attunement was there that I needed to become a fully functioning person. And while I cannot remember these earlier episodes, I can undeniably feel their lasting effects. As an adult I have realized and experienced the imprints that they have left on my life. I learned from a very early age that it was not okay to be vulnerable, and my neurological and social development suffered as a result.

Vulnerability requires that you are transparent, honest, and without defenses. This is often very difficult for people who have experienced wounding in any of these areas. Suffering repeated wounds to vulnerability can lead to addiction; this creates a barrier and insulates the addict from further pain.

The sex addict is an invulnerable creature with deeply entrenched defensive systems and an inability to trust anyone, including himself. Those who partake in behaviors and substances predominantly as a mechanism to avoid being vulnerable often find that nonintimate sex and porn best do the trick, at least temporarily, and are more easily accessible and affordable than drugs or alcohol. Also, people are exposed to sex much earlier than any other addictive substance or behavior.

It is worth noting here that many wives and husbands of sex addicts believe that their spouses were intimately bonded with the people with whom they acted out. Nothing could be further from the truth. The sex addict's inability to be vulnerable is the very thing that fuels his acting out in the first place. And since intimacy is not possible without vulnerability, it is therefore highly unlikely that a sex addict will be intimately bound to a partner with whom he is acting out.

Wounds to Authenticity

An authentic state of being is one in which a person is able to express his or her true inner self through his or her instincts and innate interests, abilities, likes, dislikes, and needs. Just as a person is born completely vulnerable, he or she is also born authentic, not yet jaded or jilted by others or the world around him or her. And just as small children are especially susceptible to wounds to their vulnerability, they are also especially susceptible to wounds to their authenticity. Many people experience these during the early vital stages in their development. Wounds to authenticity can include

- being physically or emotionally controlled;
- being told to be different than you are;

- being compared to others;
- being told you were not good enough or that you should be better than you are;
- being valued for your performance rather than your intrinsic worth;
- being forbidden or discouraged from pursuing personal dreams, goals, ideas, or interests;
- being rejected, punished, or ridiculed for being authentically you;
- being made to feel dumb or inadequate;
- being insulted about your intelligence or interests;
- not being allowed privacy, or not having personal boundaries respected by family;
- having your feelings dismissed, minimized, ignored, disregarded, shamed, or belittled by others;
- being ridiculed for your thoughts, physical appearance, or spiritual beliefs;
- being made responsible for regulating your mother's or father's emotions;
- being used as a parent's confidant;
- having emotional, physical, spiritual, creative, and mental expression stifled;
- not being allowed to develop and nurture your own interests;
- having little value placed by others on your interests or your desires;
- being forced to do your parents' will; and
- not being valued simply for being the wonderfully authentic human being that you are.

The repercussions of being wounded in any of these ways, especially early in our development, cannot and should not be understated. When we are negated, abandoned, or oppressed, or when our intrinsic worth, needs, dreams, interests, or aptitudes are seen as inferior and without value, we then learn to hide our authenticity. This means that we will begin to conform or change into what we believe people want us to be. We will feel that our authentic self is somehow flawed, and to compensate we will deny ourselves the crucial communication of expressing our needs to others. This can lead some down a path of destruction where they may begin to attempt to meet their needs compulsively through other avenues, often with addictive substances and behaviors.

Many clients report that as children, whenever they would tell the truth or simply be themselves, they would get in trouble with their parents or even be physically punished. To cope, they decided that it was a lot easier just to lie and not be their true selves. It didn't make sense to be their authentic selves if doing so would get them in trouble. Examples of this are when a child cries but is told to shut up, or if a child acts scared and is told to grow up. Children can also be punished for being too hyper, excited, silly, or joyous. Of course these kinds of suppressions to a person's authenticity don't have to occur strictly within the family unit but can also occur outside the home. A child's authentic nature can be minimized and shamed through verbal and mental bullying that happens in school or on the playground.

Another common experience that is reported by many of my clients is that nothing they did was ever good enough for their parent. I myself can relate to this.

When I was growing up, I was always compared to my brother who was a straight A student, and when my grades were only subpar, my parents would ask me, "Why can't you be more like your brother?" They would ask me the very same thing about the kid across the street: "Why can't you be more like him?" What this did was to teach me that who I was wasn't good enough. It taught me that only one thing was certain: I should attempt to be anyone but myself. It created a need inside of me to try to conform to this impossible standard of whom I should be that was set by my mother. But in reality, there was no way to accomplish that. Although a person may be able to obtain better grades or achieve more accomplishments, you can never be anyone but yourself.

The capacity to be both vulnerable and authentic is required for a person to experience intimacy. So, what is intimacy? Most people equate that word—intimacy—with sex. For example, when you hear that your friend and his girlfriend were "intimate," what immediately comes to mind? That they had sex, right? You may be correct, but true intimacy is so much more than merely having sex. It is the ability to allow others to know us fully, without reservation, and to see us at our best and at our worst. With real intimacy, we feel emotionally safe because in a true partnership there are no secrets and no lies. Now, if early adverse experiences prevent us from experiencing intimacy because we are unable to be vulnerable and authentic, parts of our brain and nervous system can be dramatically altered, hindering our capacity for true intimacy. All of this can work together to create a perfect storm that can lead a person to attempt to self-soothe with addictive substances and behaviors. And since these woundings usually occur from such a young age and sex is often the first source of self-soothing one finds, it is safe to say that these wounds can easily lead a person to use sexual behaviors as a coping mechanism.

Sex addiction is the result of a complex developmental process, and although the reasons we become addicts are diverse, the underlying ADEs are common factors. Attunement and attachment were absent, which led to the chain reaction of the inability to be vulnerable and authentic. If you weren't allowed to be vulnerable, and if your needs weren't tended to while you were vulnerable, then that is going to set you up for addiction. It's going to gear you toward seeking outside sources for self-regulation.

Self-regulation is our unconscious or involuntary response to the feelings we experience when our unresolved adverse developmental experiences are triggered. It is an automatic response to neglect, meaning that when we did not have a stronger system provided to us by a caretaker or similar figure to help guide and form our developing emotional systems, we had to find alternative ways to do so on our own. Self-regulation is associated with avoidant or anxious-avoidant attachment styles. Those of us who experienced this type of attachment learned quickly that if our needs were going to be met, then we had to meet them on our own. We learned to calm and soothe ourselves by whatever means possible, and in many cases it is only a matter of time before a person discovers either behaviors or substances that produce a chemical intoxication as a means of dealing with the inability to recognize, resolve, regulate, or express our own emotions. ADEs set us up with automatic defense systems that force us to become "self-centered," not in a selfish way, but in a protective way. In other words, we are forced to become responsible for our own emotional regulation, safety, survival, and pain management. We become self-regulated.

When early attempts at connection or self-expression leave people vulnerable to experiencing pain, they learn to rely on their own means to regulate their internal worlds. One major sacrifice we make when we self-regulate is that we are so busy managing our own system that we do not have the capacity to allow others in.

Sex addiction is an intimacy disorder, meaning those who suffer from sex addiction have little or no capacity to form long-lasting intimate bonds with others. Intimacy requires vulnerability and authenticity, and for the addict, there are just too many wounds blocking the ability to trust. Since intimacy has threatened the addict's safety in the past, any inclination of possible intimacy in the present can act as a trigger, sending signals to and causing an uproar in the body's nervous system. When this occurs, self-regulation comes back online with the purpose of protecting the addict from getting hurt again like he or she was hurt in the past. Thus, the sex that an addict seeks in order to self-regulate is anything but intimate.

Once formed, self-regulation is just that: automatic. When we act out as a means of self-regulation, we do so without thinking, driven as if on autopilot, because we are. There is a neurological process that drives self-regulation that we will begin breaking down in the next chapter. Simply stated, the brain is an incredibly efficient machine with a cortical region, out of which we act with logic and reasoning, and subcortical (lower) regions, out of which we act with instinct. While our cortical region requires large quantities of energy (glucose and oxygen) to perform adequately, our subcortical regions require only very little amounts of energy to operate. Because of the extra energy it requires to move from one's subcortical regions to one's cortical region, instead of thinking clearly, we humans often find ourselves stuck down in our instinctual brain, especially during times of stress. This is the main reason why addicts, when triggered, can stay stuck in their instinctual brains, using behavior to self-regulate. In fact, one of the most difficult tasks recovering addicts must perform is to reach out for help when they are triggered to act out. Many partners, sponsors, friends, and family members are left baffled when the addict relapses without simply reaching out. But when an addict is acting out as a means of self-regulation, he simply is not able to make rational decisions, such as dialing up a friend. In fact, we addicts have a name for this: we call it the ten-thousand-pound telephone. In 1935, at the formation of Alcoholics Anonymous, the organization coined the acronym HALT, which stands for hungry, angry, lonely, and tired. When an addict is having the inclination to relapse, he is advised instead to stay still and scan his body for any emotional or physical reasoning that may be the true culprit of the trigger. New members are instructed to HALT as often as possible in order to ward off the possibility of a slip or relapse. What the founders of AA probably didn't know in 1935 is that what they were actually doing was encouraging addicts to take a moment to muster up the extra energy that it takes to get back into their cortical brain where sound reasoning exists.

Many ask if there is a habitual component to acting out, and the answer is yes. When we repeatedly rely on ourselves through self-regulation to solve all of our problems, our behaviors become routine or habitual. We are functioning from the lower subcortical regions of our brains and are therefore more likely to ignore rational thought. Addiction is not an excuse for bad behavior, and addicts are not responsible for becoming addicts. Addiction is simply a subcortical response to a real or imagined threat that causes our thinking brain to malfunction, and it is our early environments that shape our neurological systems.

When a person is subjected to trauma at an early age in any of the forms that have been discussed here, that person can become prone to living more often in the subcortical, or instinctual, brain. Addiction is self-regulation, an attempt to keep our internal environment consistent. While some people can self-regulate using the chemicals that we naturally receive from our own brains, other people get hooked on using outside substances or behaviors that produce a similar calming, regulatory response.

Early trauma and adverse developmental experiences such as the ones that have been described thus far and that damage a person's ability to be vulnerable can also damage a person's core sense of self. They can cause a person to shut him- or herself off from others and to adopt alternative, nonauthentic ways of being. Under these conditions it is not uncommon for a person to take on a survivalist view of the world. By looking at the ways in which a person was responded to as a child, one can gain insight into how that person will grow to respond to events and people as an adolescent and into adulthood. Pat Ogden, co-author of *Trauma and the Body: A Sensorimotor Approach to Psychotherapy*, notes

> A person, a child, even an infant, will abandon actions or distort actions that are not effective in producing the desired outcome. For example, proximity-seeking actions—such as eye contact, seeking proximity, reaching out—those actions, if they are not met effectively by the attachment figures, they start to become distorted and they actually shape the person's movement patterns…we're looking at those actions that were abandoned, as well as the beliefs that were formed and the strong attachment-related emotions, that really weren't regulated by attachment figures. (quoted in Carleton 2012, 39)

Social engagement is the ability to know, understand, regulate, and express emotions in the present moment. Although every human is born with a social engagement system, a neurological system that encourages human connection, early trauma can stifle its development. "When the attachment figure is also a threat to the child," notes Ogden. (quoted in Carleton 2012, 39), "two systems with conflicting goals are activated simultaneously or sequentially: the attachment system, whose goal is to seek proximity, and the defense system, whose goal is to protect. In these contexts, the social engagement system is profoundly compromised and its development interrupted by threatening conditions."

In other words, early adverse experiences and especially trauma that involved neglect from a caregiver, such as a lack of attunement, can prevent the social engagement system from coming online and operating at its full potential. TINSA contends that it is this damage to the social engagement system that predisposes sex addiction. On the subject of adverse experiences and attachment, Robert F. Anda, Vincent J. Felitti, J. Douglas Bremner, John

D Walker, Charles Whitfield, Bruce D. Perry, Shanta R. Dube and Wayne H. Gilete el al (2005, 181) write, "Early adverse experiences may disrupt the ability to form long-term attachments in adulthood. The unsuccessful search for attachment may lead to sexual relations with multiple partners, with resultant promiscuity and other issues related to sexuality."

The body-brain connection as it relates to trauma is immense and can adversely affect us for our entire lifespan. When an individual experiences trauma and does not receive the correct physiological and emotional responses from their attachment figures to resolve that trauma, it becomes unconsciously ingrained into the body and mind. These incomplete instinctual responses to a child's need to connect are stored in the body as trauma and affect future relational abilities.

> The multifaceted language of the body depicts a lifetime of joys, sorrows, and challenges, revealed in patterns of tension, movement, gesture, posture, breath, rhythm, facial expression, sensation, physiological arousal, gait, and other action sequences. These implicit, automatic physical habits, developed in a context of trauma and attachment inadequacy, can constrain the capacity to make new meaning and respond flexibly to the here and now, often turning the future into a version of the past. (Sensorimotor Institute n.d.)

As adults we can carry around emotional damage that comes from early abandonment and neglect. We may have been invaded, meaning we have been forced to submit or live a certain way in order to receive connection. We may have been oppressed, meaning that in order to receive connection, we had to abandon our authenticity; we couldn't be ourselves. We may have been rejected, meaning that our attempt to connect was met with disapproval. And there also could have been physical and sexual abuse. In all of these cases, early adverse experiences involve the complete inability to protect one's basic human rights and dignity, and if left unresolved, these traumas can become neurologically stored in one's body and mind. Psychotherapist and writer David Grand, who is widely accredited with the development of brainspotting, a form of psychotherapy that uses the field of vision to access traumatic memories, even has a name for these stored traumas: he calls them *trauma capsules*. We will be discussing stored trauma and trauma capsules more in depth in future chapters.

As mentioned at the beginning of this chapter, not everyone who experiences traumatic events is going to be affected in the same way. It is an individual's unique experience that determines whether an event is traumatic.

My brother and I have the same mother, and so we shared many of the same adverse developmental experiences growing up. However, while for my entire life I have had to deal with the negative impacts caused by these early traumas, my brother doesn't appear to have had suffered from any trauma at all.

An experience that is traumatic for one person may not be traumatic to another. Also, adverse developmental experiences are not always necessarily directed from a parent or domestic caregiver. It is possible that they can occur within a child's community, such as at school or on the playground. However, the role of a parent should not be overlooked, even in situations such as these. As children, we are always looking to our parents for guidance and protection, even in situations when they are not physically present. So if trauma or abuse happens to a child outside the home, he or she will often seek out the parents for support and guidance. However, if the parents are told about the abuse but then neglect to take action, this can cause the negative impact of the trauma to increase tenfold, because children are always looking to their parents for resolution. And it is the denial or neglect of resolution from a caregiver that can cause the most traumatic damage to a person's vulnerable nature.

The same goes for developmental environments in which the parents are left completely unaware of the abuse because the child did not feel that his or her domestic relationships created a safe enough environment for such disclosure. For example, if the trauma that one of my clients endured as a child came in the form of verbal abuse from a teacher, I ask the client why then did he not turn to Mom or Dad for help, guidance, and support? Most often the answer to this question is that my clients thought that either they would get in more trouble at home for the disclosure, or their concerns would be dismissed altogether. And so even in situations where a person was subjected to developmental trauma outside of the home, it is still usually within one's domestic environment where a lack of attunement, intimacy, and encouragement to express authenticity can really cause the most damage. To ensure proper emotional development, a child has to have a safety valve, a place where he or she can go to talk about trauma, in order for trauma to be repaired. We all need an utterly safe, compassionate, and nonjudgmental place where we can be totally authentic and vulnerable, because the lack of such an environment is how we truly become traumatized.

As it relates to addiction, what we're looking at are experiences of trauma that alter the way that the brain and the nervous system respond to the natural world. We have previously defined trauma as the negative effects that occur within the brain and body due to adverse developmental experiences. Given that our brains are moldable, we assume that the addict's brain was molded in ways that left him or her at a disadvantage in the realm of personal relationships. If genes are turned off and on through environmental experience, we do not assume that a person was "born" with this condition or somehow genetically predetermined to become an addict. Instead we assume that it is our adverse developmental experiences and our environment that affect our genes and predispose a person to addictive behaviors. When looking for the root causes of addiction, we must ask ourselves, how did our environment shape our brains to predispose us to use substances or behaviors as a means of regulating our own emotions? What were these experiences? TINSA contends that it is primarily developmental trauma, specifically in the form of early adverse experiences, that predisposes addiction. While not all sex addiction is caused by trauma, a large number of my clients have reported significant adverse developmental experiences, usually in their early childhood. And although some experts agree that not all sex addiction is caused by trauma, many other experts are quick to point out that all addiction has its roots in trauma.

Making these connections between trauma and addiction is not about assigning blame, but is instead about recognizing how this affected you. Although at first glance, it may appear that I am a proponent of pointing out parenting flaws, nothing could be further from the truth. I have fortunately never met a parent who deliberately went out of his or her way to harm a child's physical or mental health. In *Scattered Minds: The Origins and Healing of Attention Deficit Disorder*, Gabor Maté writes that "the emotional states of the parents and how they live their lives have a major impact on the formation of their children's brains, though parents cannot often know or control such subtle unconscious influences" (2000, xviii). Humans are not perfect, parents are not mind readers, and trauma and addiction are often not as much about what our parents *did* as they are about what our parents *did not do*. With that said, parents and familial environments are the most important factors in the development of healthy brain functioning and in creating the secure functioning necessary for successful relationships. If these early relationships and domestic environments are not functioning at an optimal level, that can have serious repercussions for a child's relational abilities.

In his book *Healing Trauma*, Peter Levine states,

Trauma is about loss of connection—to ourselves, to our bodies, to our families, to others, and to the world around us. This loss of connection is often hard to recognize, because it doesn't happen all at once. It can happen slowly, over time, and we adapt to these subtle changes sometimes without even noticing them. These are the hidden effects of trauma, the ones most of us keep to ourselves. We may simply sense that we do not feel quite right, without ever becoming fully aware of what is taking place; that is, the gradual undermining of our self-esteem, self-confidence, feelings of well-being, and connection to life. Our choices become limited as we avoid certain feelings, people, situations, and places. The result of this gradual constriction of freedom is the loss of vitality and potential for the fulfillment of our dreams. (2008, 9)

Adverse development experiences can have a profound effect on every aspect of a child's life. Bruce Perry, Ronnie Pollard, Toi Blaicley, William Baker et al. write,

Trauma is an experience. How is it that this experience can transform a child's world into a terror-filled, confusing miasma that so dramatically alters the child's trajectory into and throughout adult life? Ultimately, it is the human brain that processes and internalizes traumatic (and therapeutic) experiences. It is the brain that mediates all emotional, cognitive, behavioral, social, and physiological functioning. It is the human brain from which the human mind arises and within that mind resides our humanity. Understanding the organization, function, and development of the human brain, and brain-mediated responses to threat, provides the keys to understanding the traumatized child. (1995)

In a later chapter, we will delve into the neurological processes that are affected by trauma and that drive addiction. While we now understand that sex addiction is an intimacy disorder and that it is about an automatic reaction formed by trauma that repels us from healthy relationships, we must now examine how these automatic reactions formed neurologically. Although we now know where addiction originates (early in our lives through adverse developmental experiences), we must also understand how it forms if we are to truly understand the addictive process and attain recovery.

Three

CURRENT TREATMENT MODALITIES

VERSUS A NEW FRONTIER

Today's most popular addiction treatment modalities all address the addict's behavior, but when it comes to sex addiction, they simply are not enough for a lasting recovery. But why aren't they enough? It is important to examine how each of these modalities is structured in order to see where they fall short. What commonalities do they share, and what key elements are each of these current models missing? These are the questions that will be addressed to determine where therapeutic corrections can and should be made.

Behavioral Therapy

In behavioral therapy, it is said that there are three sequential elements of addiction that need to be addressed during treatment: antecedents, behaviors, and consequences. According to this model, addiction begins with *antecedents*, which are any type of major or minor occurrences that will then provoke a person to chronically partake in certain *behaviors* and eventually result in negative *consequences* that are directly related to those behaviors. If behavioral therapy truly followed this structure, it would mean that each of these three elements would be examined and carefully addressed. In theory this model is well rounded, seemingly uncovering the root causes or antecedents of a person's addiction before and above anything else. However, the reality of behavioral therapy is much different. In fact, quite often in this type of addiction therapy, the antecedents are not addressed in any depth, if at all. For example, if we look at the common protocol for a person suffering from alcoholism, under the behavioral therapy model, most therapists and treatment centers will request that the first thing their clients do is stop drinking. This is followed by and wrapped up with an in-depth analysis of what the consequences of their drinking have been for themselves and for the people they love.

While these steps are imperative components to healing and recovery, one key element is still missing, even by this model's own standards; that is, the element of uncovering the root causes or antecedents of a person's chronic harmful behaviors. Neither stopping the behavior nor looking at the consequences of these behaviors alone has ever or will ever work as a foundation of long-term recovery. In fact it is most likely that you, the reader, have already attempted sobriety by adhering to a treatment model similar to the one just described. However, had simply stopping the behavior been able to stop your addiction, then you would probably not be reading this book. Likewise, had reviewing the consequences been able to stop your addiction, you would again most likely not be reading this book. The truth is that many therapists who claim to adhere to the behavioral therapy model often do not follow the original structure of the model. Instead, what we see is the absence of the analysis of the antecedents. Paradoxically, an in-depth review of the antecedents or root causes of addiction has been found to be the most crucial element needed to ensure long-term healing.

Most problems can be resolved by first finding out where and why the problem initially originated. In treating people with addictions, we must look at the early commonalities between addiction cases in order to understand what causes addiction. A close review of the common events that occurred early in the lives of all addicts is the answer to establishing a concrete cure for addiction. Only by uncovering the true antecedents of addiction can we really begin to resolve the problem.

Talk Therapy

The second of the three current addiction therapies being offered is known as talk therapy, a top-down approach that is more or less an environment in which people are encouraged to vocalize their addictive struggles or to "talk it out." One of the primary goals of this model is to help the addict gain access to the feelings and emotions that surround the addictive behavior. The belief is that if a therapist can get clients to talk about their problems, then it is also possible to simultaneously enable them to tap into their emotions, and from there, the healing process can begin. Unfortunately, a fundamental flaw in this way of thinking is that many people who struggle with addiction cannot simply access their emotions just by talking about their issues.

As previously mentioned, most if not all addicts report enduring some type of traumatic experience or experiences in their past. Dutch psychiatrist Bessel van der Kolk, author of *The Body Keeps the Score* (2014), has been widely acknowledged for his research in the area of posttraumatic stress since the 1970s. His work focuses on the relationship between attachment and developmental traumas and neurobiology. The book highlights his research and knowledge regarding how the brain is shaped by traumatic experiences, and he stresses the importance of integrating these findings into trauma therapies and healing practices. In his research with functional MRIs, Van der Kolk showed that when people are experiencing trauma, the frontal areas of their brain shut down. Furthermore, the frontal left cortex known as Broca's area, which is responsible for speech, is completely roadblocked and sent offline. When you also take into account the fact that trauma is stored in the lower parts of the brain, you can begin to understand the inadequacies of talk therapy.

The reason that talk therapy is referred to as a "top-down" approach is that talking about a problem generally involves only the top part of the brain known as the frontal lobe, or the thinking part of the brain. The lower parts of the brain (the limbic and the reptilian complex, or subcortical parts of the brain) are generally not involved in this process. What is interesting about this is that it is in these lower parts of the brain where the true "feelings" (or more accurately a person's innate sensory wirings) are actually stored. According to trauma specialist Peter Levine, addicts cannot change emotions because they are so "shut down" that they cannot get in touch with their feelings.

Our brains are largely an extension of our nervous systems and can become greatly affected by our experiences, most especially our early environmental surroundings. If these experiences include any traumatic wounds, it can have an enormous effect on a person's brain and nervous system and can predispose a person to addiction. So, because past traumatic experiences are often stored in the lower parts of the brain, talk therapy isn't going to do much to clean up the bottom brain mess left behind by early adverse experiences. In order to enable an addict to gain any actual long-term and sustainable recovery from his addictions, what really needs to be done is to turn therapy sessions like these upside down. If the problem really begins in the lower parts of our brain, a bottom-up approach would be much more effective, as therapists would actually be working with the areas of the brain that have been altered and rewired to drive a person to act out chronically and compulsively in harmful ways.

When we do not work with the systems that have been affected by trauma, those damaged systems remain unresolved, as does the addiction. Quite simply, you can't resolve a past trauma by talking about it. The fundamental components of how a person's brain operates when it has been damaged by traumatic events simply do not allow for that possibility. In fact, forcefully tapping into a person's emotions involving past traumatic woundings can cause enormous harm. Peter Levine best describes how disordered talk therapy can be and how it can cause even more harm than good:

> When the therapist encourages the client to talk about their trauma, asking questions such as, "Okay, so this is what happened to you. Now, let's talk about it," or, "What are you feeling about that?" The client tries to talk about it. And if they try to talk about it, they become more activated. Their brainstem and limbic system go into a hyper-aroused state, which in turns shuts down Broca's area, so they really can't express in words what's going on. They feel more frustrated. Sometimes the therapist is pushing them more and more into the frustration. Eventually the person may have some kind of catharsis, but that kind of catharsis is due frequently to being overloaded and not being able to talk about it, being extremely frustrated. (2013)

Twelve-Step Programs (Abstinence-Based Programs)

The final mainstream treatment modality for addiction that is currently available is certainly the most widely known and may be the most popular. This modality comes in the form of abstinence-based programs, more widely known as twelve-step programs.

In the mid-1980s, I entered into this type of addiction treatment via Alcoholics Anonymous for alcoholism and drug abuse and began to work through a twelve-step program. First and foremost, what I can say about Alcoholics Anonymous is that it honestly saved my life. It was the first time I had ever been immersed in an environment where I was surrounded by other people who were suffering from the same problems that I was. It was there that I learned that my addictions were not about alcohol at all, but instead they were about the problems hidden beneath the alcohol.

It was around this time in the mid-1980s that abstinence-based programs, including the twelve-step program, began to look at the family of origin. There was a great focus on inner-child work, which was a step in the right direction for addiction therapy, but I was always put off by the fact that a great deal of blame was placed on a person's parents. In fact, for several years I rigorously worked through multiple therapies, workshops, and seminars, each of which seemed to be mostly focused on helping me to uncover just how horrible my parents were. I was encouraged to blame them and to accuse them for my addiction. In the short term, it felt good to hold them responsible for how my life had become a mess, but over time deflecting the responsibility for my behaviors onto someone else only made me feel worse. It felt like a cop-out. In the long run, holding my parents responsible for my addiction and blaming others did not give me any inner peace.

As I continued my way through the twelve steps, I stumbled upon what I consider another shortcoming of the program. At the same time that I began to control the ability to stay sober from drugs and alcohol, I also became provoked by something that I could only describe as my inner addictive beast, and let me tell you, that beast was feeling quite deprived. Even though I was now able to put down the bottle, I was not able to "calm my beast" or calm my nerves, and I quickly became inclined to act out in other ways. Quite simply, I changed addictions. I often joke that if you scratch an alcoholic, you will find another addiction underneath. For me that addiction was sex. While I was most likely a sex addict before I got sober from alcohol, without the bottle, sex became my one and only nerve-calming resource. It was the only numbing potion I had left, and I began to use it in excess to try to resolve my lingering inner turmoil. The worst part about this was that in my sex addiction, I found myself going against my morals and values much more so than I ever did in my alcoholism. I also found sex addiction to be a much heavier burden to bear and a much harder addiction to contain. I found myself unable to stop my sexual behaviors in spite of adverse consequences, in spite of the risk it posed to my career and reputation, and in spite of a growing sense of isolation and loneliness.

At this point I began to understand that the twelve steps had failed to fully heal my addiction. Later, as I embarked on my own quest for answers, I discovered that the twelve steps were missing a crucial element of treatment. Through intense research in the areas of addiction and neurobiology, I later learned that long-term, substantial recovery from addiction was not possible without finding and resolving the root causes of my addictive behaviors. The inner-child work that I was encouraged to do in the twelve steps (and that I found to be a very small part of this otherwise extensive and helpful program) barely scratched the surface of the work that really needed to be done in order to understand my addiction. I needed to understand how my brain and nervous systems were affected. I needed to understand that there were ways in which to regain control over these systems in the present moment. And I needed to stop placing blame on my parents or anyone else. While to this day I contend that twelve-step recovery is absolutely essential for long-term recovery, I have also come to realize that addressing the cause and conditions that formed the addiction in the first place is just as important.

The fact is that within all three of these types of therapies (behavioral therapy, talk therapy, and abstinence-based programs), there's a high recidivism rate no matter which type of addiction is being treated. It was only through my training with sex addiction specialist Patrick Carnes that my eyes were truly opened to the deficiencies of these narrow-sighted models, all of which usually treat only one addiction at a time. I saw that within these modalities, a person was treated primarily for alcoholism, or for an eating disorder, or for sex addiction, et cetera, but not many therapists or treatment centers would ever treat a person for multiple addictions at the same time. This seemed absurd to me, as I was well aware by this point in my life that all of my addictions were absolutely interrelated. In fact, I learned that there was even a term for this: addiction interaction disorder. I knew that there must be one underlying cause stringing all of my addictions together, and, as I saw it, the problem with all of the current treatment modalities was that they neither identified nor treated that one underlying cause. These therapists and recovery programs never really got to the core of the addiction or addictions. They would treat the symptoms so that one particular addiction went into remission, but the *whole* addiction, the underlying cause of the addiction, was never resolved, leaving an addict to pick up another addiction.

These three common modalities for treating addiction do not address the root cause of addiction, nor do they give addicts any insight into what is happening to them anatomically, within their brains and their nervous systems. It is these very shortcomings that inhibit the long-term healing that is so obviously absent from these current modalities. In order to overcome the widespread problem of addiction, therapy must evolve. We must address the root causes of addiction and take steps to provide understanding about how they can affect a person's inner wirings and make that person susceptible to addictive behaviors. Once we can do that, we can begin to disarm addiction at its very core, and long-term healing will be possible.

We are, fortunately, in an exciting time in which addiction therapies are gradually moving from the behavioral approaches just described to more comprehensive methods that understand and treat the causes. Over the past twenty years, thanks to impressive advancements in science and technology, we have been able to gain so much more insight into how the brain can become altered by different scenarios, such as when it undergoes trauma, or when it is stimulated by a substance or behavior.

These findings have given us a solid foundation on which to better understand how a person can become inclined toward addiction. Listed below are a few of these major game-changing therapeutic advancements:

- CT scans, PET scans, and SPECT scans, which were introduced as an aid to scientific research, enabled researchers to see what was going on in the brain rather than just having to guess. Using these new technologies, researchers were able to track what was occurring during times of traumatic recall, as in people with posttraumatic stress disorder (PTSD). We could now begin to understand how certain behaviors were neurologically provoked and even predict how a person was going to react to future stimuli. A few of the brilliant minds and key players who were involved in gathering this early data included Daniel Siegel, Bruce Perry, and Gabor Maté.

- In 2011 renowned neuroscientist Stephen Porges published *The Polyvagal Theory: Neurophysiological Foundations of Emotions, Attachment, Communication, and Self-Regulation*, a written work that included his groundbreaking polyvagal theory of the nervous system. This theory specifies two functionally distinct branches of the vagus, or tenth cranial nerve: the dorsal vagal and the ventral vagal complex. The theory provides powerful insight into the mechanics of the brain when it undergoes stress or trauma, and it has stimulated research and progressive treatments for many different disorders, including addiction, by emphasizing the importance and influence of behavioral regulation.

When I began training to become a sex addiction therapist, I saw many common indicators and factors that would later be interwoven into my own practice. Of particular interest was Patrick Carnes's 1992 study, in which he found that 97 percent of addicts were at some point in their past emotionally abused, 87 percent were at some point physically abused, and 82 percent were sexually abused. Hearing these statistics, I knew with absolute certainty that recovering from addiction was about so much more than just attending meetings and attempting to stop a certain substance or behavior. And while, just as in the twelve steps, I was shown how a person's parents and family of origin can absolutely play a role in predisposing them to addiction, I also learned that what my parents, family, or other early influences did or did not do for me was not as important as knowing and understanding how my brain and my nervous systems were thereby affected. I was not taught to place blame on others, but instead I was given a platform on which to take responsibility for and own my addiction.

In 2008, after completing my studies with Carnes, I opened my own treatment center to help those who were suffering predominantly from sex and porn addiction. My intention was to incorporate all of my knowledge of addiction and trauma into my practice. I wanted to provide healing to anyone who walked into my office and was suffering from uncontrollable compulsive behaviors. I believed that it was possible to do this through exposing my clients to the *why* of sexual addiction. Although in the beginning I was still a bit unsure about my own hypotheses, I quickly began to see the very commonalities among my clients that I had suspected I would. I began to hear very similar stories from one patient to the next. Each individual spoke to me about adverse childhood or developmental experiences. Each individual said that he had experienced some kind of disconnection in his youth and minimal emotional support within his family of origin. They reported that they were unable to express their emotions, either because they weren't permitted to, or because they didn't know how to, due to the fact that they weren't taught how to properly regulate their emotions. While some of my clients reported extreme emotional, physical, or even sexual abuse, every single one of my clients across the board reported that someone within his family of origin (usually Mom or Dad) did not provide a way for him to emotionally express himself or to adequately handle, resolve, or identify emotions. In short, I quickly found that the majority of my clients who were suffering from sex and pornography addiction were all products of homes where unhealthy forms of attachment existed.

Discovering these commonalities was just the beginning. It didn't take long to find out that addressing these deep-seated issues with my clients was not an easy task. Apparently, many people were confused about what unhealthy attachment even meant. Many people equated material support with emotional support as it related to their upbringing. Many of my clients were quick to overshadow their emotional deprivations, citing that they were given the best clothes, the best food, or the best education. I would often have to explain to some of my clients that, while providing a child with the things necessary for survival, such as food, clothes, and shelter, is important, emotional support can be just as vital to the child's well-being. It often took a bit of work to help a patient see where the emotional support was absent from his childhood. I would have a patient initially come in and report having had a perfect childhood, yet after I asked about what had occurred around him regarding emotional expression and emotional regulation, it was as if the patient was having an epiphany even in cases like these, with clients who at first did not recognize the emotional deprivation that occurred within their childhood, this concept of unhealthy attachment quickly began to resonate with them.

It was during this time that I began to understand the difference between healthy and unhealthy attachment, and more importantly, attunement, and what these types of things really meant. A caregiver's proper emotional responses to a child's needs (attunement) as well as the feeling of being protected by that caregiver (secure/healthy attachment) are essential for proper neurological and anatomical development. New research was being conducted that identified environmental factors as being the likely catalyst that can predispose a person to addiction. This was a stark contrast to the earlier assumption that addiction was genetically inherited. In other words, nurture truly was more influential than nature.

A key figure in this realm of progressive addiction therapy research, and the person responsible for many of the advancements that were made at this time, is Dr. Gabor Maté. For the past twenty years, much of his research has been heavily focused on trauma as it relates to the brain and nervous systems and as a catalyst for addiction, about which he has stated,

> Not all addictions are rooted in abuse or trauma, but I do believe they can all be traced to painful experience. A hurt is at the center of all addictive behaviors. It is present in the gambler, the Internet addict, the compulsive shopper and the workaholic. The wound may not be as deep and the ache not as excruciating, and it may even be entirely hidden—but it's there. As we'll see, the effects of early stress or adverse experiences directly shape both the psychology and the neurobiology of addiction in the brain. (2010, 38)

Through studying these new advancements made by trauma and addiction specialists like Maté and others, along with my own findings of the commonalities among addicts, I concluded that addiction seemed to be secondary to adverse developmental experiences. These adverse developmental experiences often occurred in the form of attachment or attunement wounds, meaning that a child's nonverbal requests or emotional needs were not met. While behavioral therapy, talk therapy, and abstinence-based programs primarily concern themselves with submission to symptoms, simple behavioral tasks alone were shown to be far less effective at healing addiction than treating these causes and conditions that seemed to predispose a person to addiction in the first place. In fact, I found that when the causes and conditions were treated, the behaviors became less of a need, making abstinence inherently easier. It was here at the crossroads of a new frontier of progressive addiction research that a new treatment model for sex addiction was formed. I call this model TINSA: trauma-induced sexual addiction.

TINSA proposes that not only is sex addiction secondary to adverse developmental experiences, but more specifically these adverse developmental experiences negatively affect the brain and nervous systems in such a way that people with ADEs are propelled to rely on self-regulation as a means of maintaining control of these systems. Based on the work of many prominent neuroscientists and trauma specialists, TINSA's basic premise is that sexually compulsive behaviors are a primary indicator that damage has occurred within the autonomic nervous system's attachment and protection systems. TINSA looks at the formation of addiction, and more specifically sex addiction, through a neurobiological lens and uses this information to treat sufferers. Simply stated, rather than merely using the existing abstinence and behavioral methods that on their own continue to fail, TINSA treats the cause and the core of addiction to ensure long-term recovery.

When I was attending Alcoholics Anonymous meetings, I would often hear that it doesn't matter what happened in the past; what matters is how you're going to stay sober. Contrary to that methodology, I believe that what happened in the past matters a lot because it is pivotal to future behaviors. What occurs in a person's life, especially at a young age, can greatly alter how current events and information are neurologically processed. If a person experiences adverse childhood experiences, these traumas can shift how that person will respond and behave in certain situations later in life. Unless that person can understand how and why these shifts occur, true healing is not possible. Until an addict becomes educated on how the brain and nervous system can become damaged and rewired as a result of past traumas, that person will remain at the mercy of his addiction(s).

The TINSA models use interpersonal neurobiology to explain the formation and treatment of sexual addiction. Addictions, whether to a substance such as alcohol, drugs, or food, or a behavior such as sex, gambling, or shopping, all share the same neurological pathways. The only difference is that substance addictions rely on sources outside of the body, while behavioral addictions rely on behavioral rituals to engage their own neural chemistry. And when it comes to engaging one's own neural chemistry, sex addicts in particular are master chemists. We unconsciously experiment with a broad range of behaviors to find the perfect cocktail to control and regulate our pain. Then, just as the alcoholic chooses his or her favorite beverage, the sex addict will repeatedly return to a particular behavior or sequence of behaviors, becoming more and more reliant upon that particular behavior or sequence of behaviors each time. Understanding exactly how sexual behaviors can be used in this way, to manipulate a person's own neurochemistry in order to regulate pain, is all part of TINSA's modality.

Foundation of Regulation
Triune Brain & Autonomic Nervous System Correlation

Sympathetic Limbic System Fight/Flight Unconscious

Social Engagement Neocortex Frontal Lobe Present/Safe/Aware Conscious

Parasympathetic Reptilian Complex Freeze Unconscious

The primary tool that TINSA uses to understand, explain, and treat sex addiction is the foundation of regulation, to describe the zone of arousal in which a person experiences optimal autonomic functioning. When a person stays within the limits of this zone, the brain is said to be properly functioning and in balance. Within this zone, the emotional brain and the rational brain are able to work together in harmony to provide us with feelings of safety, connection, and receptivity and with the capacity for social engagement. Here we are able to process information and respond appropriately to everyday situations with ease. We are able to think rationally and make sensible decisions. But every so often, people can be thrust out of this safety zone and find themselves either above or below the foundation in states of either hyper- or hypo-arousal. While this can happen to any person (not just addicts) at any time as a result of extreme stress, for most individuals (those with healthy neurological functioning), it does not happen very often. In fact, most humans remain within their foundations for most of their lives. For others, it isn't so easy. In later chapters we will explore the structure and functionality of the foundation of regulation, its three different compartments, and how we are affected by it.

Another key component to understanding and treating sexually compulsive behaviors is a true understanding of the equation introduced in chapter 1: vulnerability plus authenticity equals intimacy. If a person is within the safe confines of his or her foundation of regulation, then that person is able to be vulnerable. While every human being begins life this way, with a foundation vastly equipped with the ability to express vulnerability, we are also fragile and susceptible to adverse experiences that can threaten that ability. It is only through wounds to our vulnerable nature that we learn to close off and adopt certain defense mechanisms, even to the detriment of our own health. And in the same way that we are all born innately vulnerable, we are also all born authentic, absolutely complete, and perfect as we are. However, when from a young age our authenticity is not allowed or is shamed or deemed unacceptable, we often cope by forming a separate persona, one that is more likely to receive acceptance and validation.

For those of us whose authenticity was rejected in this way and whose vulnerability was damaged, we become incapable of forming intimate, deeply connected relationships as adults. We form a deeply flawed belief system about ourselves, relationships, and the world. We seek our worth through possessions, through other people, or through accomplishments. We feel that we have built a life suitable for other people, but not for ourselves. Wounds to our vulnerability and authenticity create a basic mistrust of the world. We become closed off and believe we have to take care of ourselves. We become masters of regulating our own mood, often preferring to be numb. And we are constantly on guard, scanning for people, places, and situations that could hurt us while we are in a vulnerable or authentic state.

These are just some of the realities and ways of being that addicts report experiencing every day. If you are an addict, then these agonizing forms of existence resonate deeply with you, and you have most likely adopted similar defense and coping mechanisms that have become a way of life. It is well documented that sexual addiction is an intimacy disorder, which by definition is the complete inability to form a vulnerable, authentic, and transparent relationship with another human being. While intimacy-disordered individuals are certainly capable of forming relationships that *appear* deep, in truth these relationships are terribly shallow due to the individual's inability to ever let a partner intimately know his true self. In fact, addicts believe that no one has ever really known them. Faced with pain and shame, these people go the distance to protect themselves at all costs, including closing themselves off from the intimacy that every human being is wired to receive.

TINSA's success as a healing modality can be attributed to its attention to the antecedents and root causes of a person's inability to express intimacy. Under the TINSA model, the first step is to gauge the patient's ability to live within his foundation. After that we look for any adverse developmental experiences that may have decreased the patient's ability to live within his foundation. This is where sex addiction and intimacy disorders can always be traced back to developmentally traumatic experiences that happened to a person in early childhood. In some cases these experiences may have occurred within the community or in school, but most often they occurred within the family of origin, and more specifically, within the person's relationship to his mother or father. Even in cases where clients reported only having adverse experiences at school or on the playground, these experiences were often coupled with a lack of attunement at home. If the trauma that a person experienced as a child occurred outside of the home, ideally that trauma would have been able to be repaired within the family of origin and by that person's primary caregivers. The single most important component of proper neurological growth and functioning is that from a young age, a child is given correct attunement and healthy attachment within a safe, compassionate, and nonjudgmental domestic system. In other words, adverse childhood experiences of any type have the ability to be cured and avoided as long as the child has a home environment in which he or she is able to be totally authentic and vulnerable. The father who hugs his crying son rather than telling him to "man up" and stop bawling after a Little League strikeout is giving his child the attunement and attachment needed to grow and develop in positive ways. If a child grows up within an environment where this is not the case, then that can set him or her up to be prone to addiction later in life.

TINSA's premise that trauma is the primary catalyst for sex addiction is, of course, met with skepticism by some experts in the field. While it is true that the science that supports this theory is still emerging, there is much evidence that shows the damage that trauma can do to the brain, as well as a multitude of statistics that show that most people who are prone to addiction also experienced some sort of childhood trauma. As mentioned earlier, due to the increased accessibility and proliferation of Internet pornography, along with the well-documented influx of those who associate with this disorder, sex addiction is undeniably an epidemic that is rapidly escalating. Therefore, it is extremely important that we start to recognize the legitimacy of the progressive trauma and addiction research that has been done and continues to be done so that we can finally begin to treat sex addiction with a properly structured modality that will once and for all provide long-term recovery.

TINSA is not the first theory to recognize that sex addiction might be caused by early traumatic woundings. This way of thought can be traced as far back as 1985, when Patrick Carnes was producing research indicating that those who suffer from sexual addiction had also experienced some sort of developmental trauma. Other major contributors include Bessel van der Kolk, Gabor Maté, and Pat Ogden. In fact, there is a full and bountiful history of documentation that hypothesizes the correlation of early trauma and sexual addiction. However, this book proposes that TINSA is the first and only model to extensively break down that correlation and to identify and treat the specific damage that occurs from these developmental traumas. Generally speaking though, primarily focusing on the treatment of past trauma as a means of recovery from addiction is still widely regarded as an avant-garde therapeutic approach. And while there will continue to be skeptics, this type of progressive treatment is the only current modality that actually works to heal sex addiction.

Addicts are very interested to discover the correlation between their adverse developmental experiences and their addiction. When they become knowledgeable about the physical alterations that occurred within their neurological and nervous systems because of these past experiences, they are able to break free of the shame that they have carried with them for so long. Explaining how the brain and nervous system are involved in the addictive process and cycle enables addicts to remain calm in stressful, triggering situations and gives them a regained sense of control.

We cannot resolve trauma through behavioral approaches or talk therapy or abstinence-based programs alone because these modalities are not getting to the core of what is really going on. While abstinence and behavioral therapies are important, they are not realistic for long-term sobriety because they aren't equipped to combat a damaged neurological system. You have to do actual work that is going to access the midbrain and the lower brain. That includes methods such as eye movement desensitization and reprocessing (EMDR), brainspotting, somatic experience (SE), sensorimotor psychotherapy, and dialectical behavioral therapy—all of which will be discussed in later chapters.

Over the next few chapters, I will be contributing my own empirical evidence to a growing body of research that contends that sexual addiction is secondary to adverse developmental experiences. I will explain how early adverse experiences actually mold our brain and nervous systems to color all of our future experiences. By combining my own findings with the research established by the world's leading experts in trauma, I will attempt to provide the reader with an in-depth, coherent explanation of the cause, progression, and restitution of sexual addiction. It is my hope that by seeing these root causes of sex addiction brought to light, millions of people who suffer from their compulsive sexual behaviors may decide to seek treatment and actively work toward healing. Because there is hope and there is a way out.

Four

The Brain and Addiction:

The Dopamine Factor

As previously discussed, talk therapy and abstinence- or behavioral-based tools cannot, in and of themselves, give addicts the ability to sustain long-term healing. The core issues behind addiction must be addressed. A substantial amount of empirical evidence and research shows how adverse developmental experiences can affect our brains and nervous systems and can predispose a person to addiction. These experiences need to be incorporated into therapy. This is where TINSA was born, a treatment modality that gives clients access to an in-depth analysis of these findings.

Part of TINSA's basic premise is that an addict can firmly establish remission if given the knowledge and insight into how the addiction initially formed (and continues to be used) as a way to regulate damaged anatomical systems. Once an addict can comprehend how the addiction is used in this way, as a sort of survival mechanism, then the healing process can begin. Through complete understanding of how early trauma can adversely affect the brain and nervous systems, an addict can then use alternative, healthier methods of mending and regulating these damaged systems.

Swiss psychologist Alice Miller (2009, 126) says that addiction "is a sign, a signal, a symptom of distress. It is a language that tells us about a plight that must be understood." We've known for years that a hijacked brain, one that has been automatically taken over by its lower compartments and is no longer operating out of its frontal lobe, is linked to addiction. This hijacking of the brain can happen in almost any human being during times of emotional distress. However, a person with a brain that functions healthily overall will experience this hijacking mechanism far less frequently than a person whose neurobiological system has been damaged by past trauma. Both the brain and nervous system can be adversely affected and damaged by trauma, and it is under these conditions that a person can become susceptible to partaking in addictive substances and behaviors.

To understand addiction, we must first understand the inner workings of the body's neurobiological systems; in this way, we can then quite literally get to the root of addiction. Humans are evolutionary creatures in that our brains and nervous systems developed over time. To fully understand their makeup (and thereby comprehend addiction), it is important to have some rudimentary understanding of the basic components of both the model of the triune brain and the polyvagal theory of the nervous system. In this chapter we begin by breaking down the body's mastermind—the brain—to uncover how past trauma can detrimentally alter the way it functions.

The Triune Brain

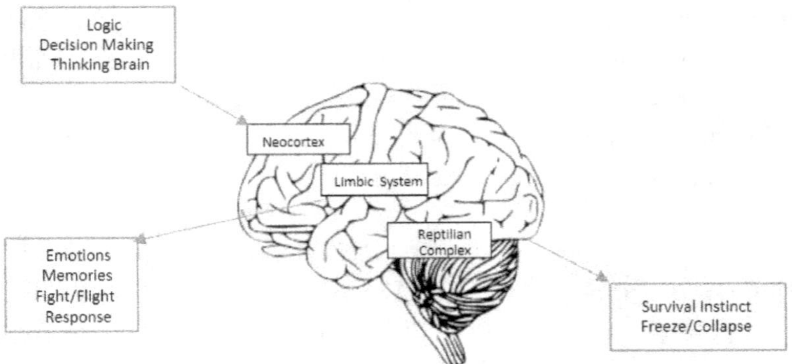

The triune brain is a model of the evolution of the brain and its behavior, as proposed by physician and neuroscientist Paul D. MacLean. MacLean showed that there exist three distinct formations of our brain, which we use in different situations for everyday survival. Our oldest brain formation is the reptilian brain; followed by the limbic system or mammalian brain; and the most recent brain formation, the frontal lobe, also called the neocortex.

Each of these structures formed, one on top of the other, at different times during our evolution to arm us with unique survival mechanisms that would be needed during that period of time. Although the brain became more advanced as we evolved, the older, more primitive brain structures can still play a large part in our thought and behavioral processes. The following sections provide detail on each formation.

The Reptilian Brain

Also called the reptilian complex, this is our most primitive brain. Developed just short of five hundred million years ago, the reptilian brain first appeared in fish and continued to advance in reptiles. This brain system is about sensation and instinctual reaction. It controls breathing, balance, and temperature regulation. TINSA hypothesizes that the reptilian complex has survival functions as well. One such mechanism is that of immobilization, or more commonly called freeze. We can see this today when we see nature programs showing lizards or similar reptiles freeze in place when threatened. This was a great survival tactic that would slow or stop them, because freezing in place would often keep one hidden from hungry predators. However, we also see this when mammals, including humans, face life-threatening situations, often reverting back to this primitive neurological system when the brain automatically acts out of instinct.

The Limbic System (the Mammalian Brain)

Later in our evolution, about 150 million years ago, the limbic system first appeared in small mammals to accompany the newfound ability to move about. These small mammals were now equipped with extremities and the capacity to fight off or flee from predators, and the limbic system developed to include expression of emotion and memory. The primary focus of the limbic brain is survival; it controls the body's response to danger. It processes short-term memory and continually scans the surrounding environment to see if we are safe. As with the reptilian brain, humans often revert to this neurological system when we act instinctively, especially if an event that is happening in the present moment is seemingly associated with a past memory.

The Frontal Lobe (the Neocortex)

The frontal lobe began its neurological formation in primates only two or three million years ago, as the genus *Homo* emerged. Just like the reptilian brain and the limbic system, this portion of the brain is meant to react to and protect us from danger. However, unlike its more primitive neighbors, the frontal lobe reacts consciously. This is because at this point in our evolution, we needed to develop a system that not only allowed for more civilized responses to threats but also allowed us to connect to others for safety. The frontal lobe provided us with a new type of social survival. It allows for our higher level of thinking, including analysis, logic, and decision making, and it is what separates us from lower-ordered animals that rely solely on instincts. Also included in this part of the brain is Broca's area, which is responsible for language and verbal communication.

In a nutshell, on the top we have our cortical brain, which comprises the frontal lobe. This is the most recently developed portion of our brain—the conscious, thinking brain. At the bottom, we have our subcortical, unconscious brain, which is made up of the limbic and reptilian complexes and is dictated by instinct and emotions and often results in knee-jerk reactions. These systems are used hierarchically. In normal everyday functioning, we will lead with our frontal lobe in an attempt to socially engage, meaning that our first line of defense is to use the neocortex and operate out of our frontal lobe. If something occurs that we perceive as threatening, we will first try to talk our way out of it, smile, or remain calm. We will use conscious thought processes to try our best not to incite anything else because we are modern, social creatures, and our survival instincts are to try to get along with other people. However, in times of intense stress or in situations that remind us of past trauma, this survival mechanism can easily be overridden by the earlier survival strategies of the mammalian and reptilian brains. If our neocortex fails to equip us with the ability to communicate and engage with others, our limbic system will take over, and we can be sent into our fight-or-flight response. Finally, if we are unable to fight our way out, or if fleeing is not an option, the most primitive line of defense employs, and we freeze, immobilize, or fully collapse. In other words, when we perceive an event or occurrence to be extremely threatening (often due to associating that event with a past memory), the frontal lobe is likely to become disengaged so that we can protect ourselves with what the brain deems in that moment to be more effective methods. This is the hijacking process, and it occurs regardless of whether the threat is real or merely perceived.

The Social Engagement System

This is the state of being at which most people function for the majority of their lives. In relation to the triune brain, social engagement is only possible when all three brains are functioning in unison (when there is a neurological sense of safety). While every person can fluctuate between using the reptilian brain, limbic system, and frontal lobe in different situations, most people more or less have optimal neurobiological functioning, meaning that they are able to stay primarily in their frontal lobe and consciously and rationally react to adverse situations. However, for people who experienced developmental trauma as children, optimal neurobiological functioning does not come so easily, and those affected by ADEs tend to resort back to using their more primitive survival instincts more often, stifling their ability to socially engage. This is because when developmental trauma occurs to someone at a very young age, especially to an infant or toddler, the only line of defense fully operational at this time is the freeze response. If a child's vocal and social distress cues are not accurately responded to by the caregiver, that child will begin to resort to using other survival mechanisms. Because they are often too young to fight their way out of a problem or flee from the problem, when infants and toddlers undergo trauma, their only manner of protection is to use their subcortical defenses, meaning they freeze, collapse, or submit in the face of adverse experiences in order to survive.

It is well recorded that the long-term effects of developmental trauma on a person's brain functionality can be monstrous. Although no one knows precisely how this damage occurs, it is widely acknowledged that early traumatic events that are too overwhelming to process in real time are instead stored as memories in the lower parts of the brain. Furthermore, these stored memories can cause dysfunction for the brain as a whole. Studies of older individuals with PTSD have shown that their hippocampus is actually smaller than those without PTSD, which may impair the processing of explicit memory. As a result, trauma may produce direct effects on the brain structures, including memory encoding, storage, and retrieval (Van der Kolk 1994).

In the case of sex addiction, early traumatic experiences have long-term effects on the way the brain works, so that reactions to everyday occurrences trigger behavior that is mostly unconscious. Traumatic memory can be activated by any sort of stimulus that awakens the memory or is in some way a reminder of that past trauma. Although science still has its limitations in this area and no one knows for sure, it is widely believed that traumatic memory is stored in the lower parts of the brain that are associated with visual and somatic memory. This means that sights, sounds, and body sensations that are happening in the present moment but may resemble those that occurred during a past traumatic event can alternatively awaken and trigger these past traumatic memories. Most people aren't aware when they are triggered in this way, however, because they aren't even aware of what their triggers are, as they have been stored and buried in their unconscious.

The overlap between a new event and stored information from an earlier event is infinitely small. Because of this, once traumatized, our brain can be hijacked, meaning that when presented with smaller and smaller threats, our emotional brain takes over to eliminate or avoid the threat.

When trauma originally occurs, implicit memories of the traumatic event are stored physiologically as emotional memories. In the beginning stages of therapy, memories are often hidden and instead expressed as sensations and emotions. Many of my clients will exhibit different body sensations and pains; shortness of breath; sweating; anxiety or feelings of immobilization, depression, or numbness; chest pains; or breathing issues, which can be deeper symptoms of traumatic events. While explicit memories are memories that have made the transition from subcortical (unconscious) to neocortical (conscious) and can therefore be more accurately pieced together, those who have suffered trauma can experience disorganized or implicit memories. Bessel van der Kolk (2014) suggests that trauma can be resolved through practices that help a person's implicit traumatic memories to become explicit. Addicts must work diligently to uncover the source of these emotional and physiological responses to past trauma. Techniques such as EMDR and brainspotting are ideal to work with the subcortical responses to trauma in order to avoid having a severe emotional flashback while uncovering these memories.

Addicts live more in their unconscious, emotional, and instinctual brains than in their frontal lobe or social engagement system. When the limbic and reptilian brain take over, the conscious brain turns off and the brain is hijacked, so we are not thinking—we are just reacting. This is why we do not worry about consequences when we are active in our addiction, because only the thinking brain has the capacity to worry. The limbic and reptilian brain just react to threats. Addiction is a dissociative disorder; when we are partaking of the substance or doing the behavior, we are not functioning optimally out of the fully evolved part of our brain. This is why when our partners ask, "Weren't you thinking of me?" the honest answer is no. When we act out, conscious thought is turned off, and everything else is out the window, including loved ones and consequences.

When the brain is hijacked, it becomes difficult for a person who has already become hooked on a behavior or substance to be able to abstain from that addictive behavior or substance. In fact, it is nearly impossible for an addict in this situation to have the capacity to do the behavioral things required to stay sober, because rational and conscious thought processes are inaccessible. For example, the addict is not likely to have the capacity to pause long enough to pick up the phone and call his or her sponsor. That type of rational thought process just isn't possible when a person is operating from the lower brains. Instead, what is much more likely to occur is that the person will act out in that moment and then call his or her sponsor later, when the thinking part of the brain, the frontal lobe, is functioning again.

The information presented here is not meant to excuse the harmful behavior of addicts. While it is important that addicts know that they are not at fault for their condition, it is equally important that they understand they are completely responsible for their behavior. The information offered in this book is provided to give addicts the necessary understanding of their own damaged neurobiological processes in order to give them the power to reposition themselves back into their social engagement system and avoid partaking of compulsive, addictive behaviors.

Early developmental trauma predisposes a person to sex addiction because at the very core, trauma is merely a disintegrated state, meaning that the three parts of the triune brain are not integrated. They cannot function together simultaneously; instead, when one system is in use, the other systems go offline. During traumatic events and occurrences, the part of the brain that is especially affected in this way and that is sent offline most frequently is the frontal lobe. This means that in times of trauma or traumatic recall, language is silenced, social communication skills are incapacitated, and the ability to remain calm and think rationally is disabled. Instead it is our primitive survival skills that take charge, sending us either into a dissociated state or a state of hyperarousal.

Daniel Goleman, author of *Emotional Intelligence* (2005), writes that it takes only milliseconds for information to come through the thalamus and reach the midbrain where, if that information is deemed threatening (whether that threat is real or imagined) or triggers a past traumatic memory, these primitive survival skills may promptly take action and override the frontal lobe. Conversely, Goleman says that it takes a much lengthier period—eight seconds—for the same information to reach and be processed by the prefrontal cortex. It is as if the conscious part of the brain never even stands a chance to process ordinary information rationally. Remember, these systems are disintegrated. When the primitive animal defenses—including fight, flight, freeze, submit, or collapse—are activated, and we are acting out of our lower and midbrain, that means that the social engagement system is not accessible.

In addition to early trauma's adverse impacts on how the brain functions, many experts in the field of addiction also contend that trauma can negatively impact the brain's production of dopamine. Bruce Perry and Ronnie Pollard (1997) have suggested that those experiencing trauma, both in utero and shortly after, actually develop fewer dopamine receptors early on in life, which can predispose a person to addiction. This deformation is directly linked and caused by adverse childhood experiences.

Addiction: Debilitated Reward Circuitry

The reward system in our brain is what processes dopamine, the body's pleasure-producing neurochemical. This system is comprised of dopamine receptors, and in a healthy, functioning brain, these receptors are able to receive and process dopamine at a normal rate, keeping us well balanced. If, however, the amount of dopamine receptors that a person has is limited, then that person will process dopamine at a limited rate. In cases like these, what this means is that ordinary but pleasurable dopamine-producing activities don't feel as good as they should. All of this can set a person up to seek more dopamine just to feel normal. Whether through pleasure-producing substances or behaviors, there are countless ways to find outside sources of dopamine, many of which can be highly addictive, as they can cause the person to become hooked on the dopamine provided. This is the very definition of addiction.

If the experts are correct, then all of this can be traced back to early trauma. Lack of attunement or bonding early on in life can prevent dopamine receptors from forming. And if a young person has fewer dopamine receptors, then from an early age that person will automatically be in pursuit of dopamine, searching for something to make him or her feel good. Oftentimes the first feel-good behavior that a child finds is through sexual stimuli. Anything that is sexual in nature, especially when discovered for the first time, is going to provide the brain with a big blast of dopamine, whether that is through television, magazines, personal fantasies, personal touch, or online pornography, which is being discovered by and is accessible to kids at an alarmingly young age. Gary Wilson (2014) notes that the teenage brain is at its peak of dopamine production, making it highly vulnerable to sex and pornography addiction and rewiring. The point is that whatever the behavior, the brain will register this initial event as a time when it finally received enough dopamine to feel normal.

For me this occurred when I was five years old, and I found the lingerie section in a JC Penney catalog. I remember this event clearly. I remember that it felt good, and for once I felt normal. My brain was finally getting enough dopamine, and so it recorded this event as a tool that I could use later on to feel good. Although I didn't come back to this type of visual sexual stimulation until years later, it did eventually become a go-to tool that I would use to escape the emotional vacancy that was occurring in my household. Of course, at only five years old, I didn't consciously record this event as a tool that I would use later on to manage my life and my emotions, but that is exactly what ended up occurring.

The first solution we find to this problem of dopamine deficiency is usually the solution that we will continually return to, and because sex is such a developmental staple for humans from such an early age, it can often become the long-term solution and go-to source of dopamine for many people. However, while sexual behaviors can work as short-term fixes by providing a large dose of dopamine to the brain, over time these behaviors can have big consequences and ultimately lead to addiction.

The biggest problem with this so-called solution is that many of these behaviors, including masturbation, pornography, and high-risk sexual activities and fantasies, induce dopamine secretion to occur in abnormally high amounts. Simply put, we do not need that much dopamine. This causes the synapses to become flooded and sends the brain into panic mode.

But the brain is very adaptable. Although the brain can't regulate the amount of dopamine coming in (because it cannot control a person's behavior or make a person stop doing a behavior) what the brain can do is regulate how much dopamine gets through. It does so through a process called *down regulation* in which, if the brain receives more dopamine than it can handle, it begins to take away or disable its dopamine receptors. It is important to note here that generally speaking, the higher the risk of the sexual behavior, the more dopamine is produced. This is why, especially into adulthood, sex addicts will often seek high-risk sexual activity, such as paying for sex or having extramarital affairs, because if sex is mixed with either fear, pain, or shame, it increases the rush, secreting higher levels of dopamine and creating greater amounts of pleasure. As our dopamine receptors keep declining and weakening, we need more and more dopamine to get the same effect. All of this can set us up to be constantly seeking higher-risk sexual activities.

This is where progression and escalation kick in. Progression is where we need more of the same thing in order to get the same effect, and escalation is when we start to change or escalate into more risky behaviors or higher-dopamine-producing behaviors in order to get the same effect. This leads to what is known as *regulation*. Instead of doing something as a means of feeling good, now we experience a dependency or need to do it just so we can feel normal. It's no longer about the high, but instead it becomes solely about overcoming withdrawals just to get back to our baseline. We need a dopamine fix to self-regulate, which initiates the pathological pursuit of rewards and relief through the use of substances and behaviors. As Gary Wilson explains,

"When dopamine receptors drop after too much stimulation, the brain doesn't respond as much, and we feel less reward from pleasure. That drives us to search even harder for feelings of satisfaction—for example, by seeking out more extreme sexual stimuli, longer porn sessions, or more frequent porn viewing—thus further numbing the brain" (2014, 58).

Chronically partaking in sexual behaviors can cause a dependency on those behaviors in the same way that regular use of any addictive substance can cause a dependency on that substance. In fact, studies have shown that orgasm has been shown to provide a blast of dopamine equivalent to a heroin rush. With these factors in mind, one must also conclude that the plethora of studies that confirm that substance abuse can lead to the aforementioned brain irregularities involving dopamine and dopamine receptor deficiency must also apply to sexual behavioral abuse. Of substance abuse and its effects on the brain that lead to addiction, Gabor Maté wrote, "Why does chronic self-administration of cocaine reduce the density of dopamine receptors? It's a simple matter of brain economics. The brain is accustomed to a certain level of dopamine activity. If it is flooded with artificially high dopamine levels, it seeks to restore the equilibrium by reducing the number of receptors where the dopamine can act. This mechanism helps to explain the phenomenon of regulation, by which the user has to inject, ingest, or inhale higher and higher doses of a substance to get the same effect as before" (2010, 152). If, in fact, sexual behavior produces dopamine in the same way that cocaine and other highly addictive substances do and as many experts now say that it does, then this is also the very same way by which chronic sexual behavior can lead to regulation, escalation, dependency, and addiction.

Furthermore, a number of studies show that adverse childhood and environmental experiences can cause these initial detrimental effects on the brain's dopamine receptors, leading to and being the catalyst for substance abuse. These findings could surely then also be applied to behavioral abuse and more specifically, sexual behavioral abuse. "Studies done on primates and other animals have shown that low social status and being dominated enhance the risk of drug use, with negative effects on dopamine receptors. By contrast, after being housed with more subordinate animals, dominant monkeys had an increase of over 20 percent of their dopamine receptors and a decrease in their tendency to use cocaine. The findings of stress research suggest that the issue is not control over others, but whether one is free to exercise control in one's own life" (Maté 2010, 318).

A major part of TINSA's premise is that the limited ability and freedom to express one's authentic self can drive a person to adopt and become addicted to sexual behaviors.

It is important to mention here that when you are young and exposed to too much pornography and sexuality, it can be extremely overstimulating. As previously mentioned, trauma is often caused by overstimulation or by the input of too much information. This is because the brain often cannot process or handle an event that is sensationally overwhelming, dense with information, or that involves too much stimulation. Gary Wilson (2014) notes that we are neither meant to see nor wired to see the amount of sexuality that occurs within pornography. In fact, just one pornographic movie is filled with more visual sexuality than all of our ancestors saw in their entire lives. Therefore, pornography itself is not only a behavior chosen to temporarily relieve trauma, but it can also be the very cause of trauma—creating a vicious cycle of reenactment and dependency.

Beyond the brain, adverse developmental experiences can also negatively impact another important anatomical system—the nervous system. In the same way that early trauma can stunt proper brain function, early trauma can also cause functional irregularities to the autonomic nervous system, and this too can ultimately lead a person to indulge incessantly in addictive substances or behaviors. In the following chapter, we will be discussing the three components of the nervous system and will uncover how both the brain and the nervous system can work together to fuel addiction.

Five

The Brain, the Autonomic Nervous System, and Our Foundations

In chapter 4 we learned how the brain works, Dr. Paul D. MacLean's theory of the triune brain, and how, when activated, each area has a particular function. To further our understanding, we will now focus on how the brain communicates these functions through our autonomic nervous system.

TINSA was born out of empirical evidence being paired with the theories of some of the greatest minds in neurology and psychology and relies heavily on Dr. Stephen Porges's polyvagal theory as well as MacLean's triune brain theory. This modality uses a graphic called the foundation of regulation to demonstrate the brain and the autonomic nervous system in simplified, visual terms (see chapter 3). Doing so enables clients to

1. see how the brain and nervous system function together;
2. understand the role of the brain and the nervous system in emotional health and in addiction;
3. understand how damage to normal functioning of the brain and nervous system predisposes individuals to self-regulation and addiction; and
4. better engage with their systems, allowing greater awareness, control, and healthy bonding and intimacy.

To understand how TINSA utilizes this foundation in treatment and recovery, we must have a basic understanding of the brain and the autonomic nervous system (ANS) and how these systems were affected, causing the individual to be predisposed to addictive behaviors.

The Autonomic Nervous System

Until Stephen Porges discovered that the parasympathetic division of the autonomic nervous system actually consists of two separate branches resulting in two different responses, scientists believed that humans only had two autonomic nervous system responses: sympathetic (fight or flight) and parasympathetic (freeze and collapse). TINSA uses Porges's discovery of three distinct responses of our autonomic nervous system to explain and give a greater understanding to our clients, giving them the ability to regulate their own systems in healthy ways for the first time.

Without going too deeply into terminology that might confound and confuse, what follows is a general outline of these three responses of the ANS so the reader can better understand TINSA's use of what I call the foundation of regulation.

As noted above, Stephen Porges discovered that there are three distinct responses of the autonomic nervous system. The sympathetic division is associated with fight or flight, and the parasympathetic division is associated with calm and rest. However, the parasympathetic system has two separate branches that consist of not one but two distinct responses. The main nerve in the parasympathetic division of the autonomic nervous system is the vagal nerve. This nerve actually contains two distinct branches, the dorsal (behind) vagal nerve, which is responsible for the freeze-and-collapse response; and the ventral (frontal) vagal, which is associated with calm, social engagement, and the ability to relate and communicate with others. This theory, which was published in the mid-1990s, describes the three responses in the development of the mammalian nervous system. Briefly stated, Porges demonstrated that our ANS comprises three distinct responses:

1. Immobilization, freeze, and collapse (dorsal branch of the vagal nerve)
2. Mobilization, fight/flight/freeze (sympathetic division)
3. Social engagement (ventral branch of the vagal nerve)

The Dorsal Vagal

Our oldest and most primitive form of defense occurs when the dorsal vagal nerve is activated. The result is behavioral shutdown, freeze, and collapse. As outlined above, this is a primitive branch of the vagus nerve, and it is shared by most vertebrates. The dorsal vagal nerve originates in the dorsal motor nucleus of our brain stem. We can see an example of the activation of this nerve in animal documentaries when a lion is chasing a gazelle, and the gazelle, knowing that it cannot fight or flee the lion, drops to the ground and appears dead.

This is not a conscious effort on the part of the gazelle but a primitive survival response. Perhaps the lion will leave the gazelle alone, thinking that it is dead, or if it decides to feast on the gazelle, this response helps to prepare the gazelle for death with minimal pain.

Sympathetic

The sympathetic division of the autonomic nervous system is associated with mobilization, or fight or flight. Activation of the sympathetic response results in increased metabolic activity and cardiac output. Our sympathetic nervous system is also known as our fight-or-flight system, enabling us to escape threat by either running away or fighting off our attacker.

Ventral Vagal

Our most recently developed autonomic nervous system response is our social engagement system. This system is the second response of our parasympathetic nervous system (the first being freeze and collapse) and is responsible for our ability to engage socially with others and navigate relationships. This system allows us to be highly attuned to other human beings and to scan our environments for safety by such measures as reading facial expressions and listening to verbal tones. The social engagement system is controlled by our ventral vagal nerve (which is a very smart nerve with a rapid response) allowing us to "know" if we are safe enough to calm our defenses through a process called neuroception (the brain's ability to sense safety). The chief function of this system is to inhibit our usually active sympathetic nervous system so that we won't go into fight, flight, or freeze, enabling us to better relate, bond, and form intimate relationships.

Within each of us there is a metaphorical foundation in which we can observe in real time the functioning of our brain and of our autonomic nervous system. Within that foundation we see the parasympathetic nervous system (dorsal and ventral vagal nerves) and the sympathetic branch of our nervous system constantly in a state of flux. Remember, ventral is associated with calm and safety; sympathetic with fight, flight, or freeze; and dorsal with freeze, immobilization, and eventually collapse.

Sympathetic (fight/flight/freeze)
Ventral Vagal (calm/safety)
Dorsal Vagal (freeze/submit/collapse)

If all goes well and as expected in our daily lives, we can stay within our foundation by self-regulation, utilizing our ventral vagal response. If, however, there is a threat, our sympathetic branch will be activated and take us out of our foundation, placing us into a state of either fight or flight. We will either angrily lash out or find a way to run away, depending on how large the threat is. It is important to remember that threats can be real or imagined, but our bodies will react in exactly the same way. Those of us with ADEs are more likely to have many more threats than those who did not experience ADEs or who had them resolved.

Should the sympathetic system be able to extinguish the threat (real or imagined), then our ventral vagal will reengage, bring us back into our foundation, and provide us with a sense of safety. If, however, the threat cannot be extinguished by running away or fighting, our dorsal vagal will activate and throw us into a state of freeze or shutdown, submission, and eventually collapse, leaving us with no ability to respond.

Using TINSA's term *foundation* allows clients to see their current state of autonomic (automatic) functioning. A great deal of relief can be provided when a person in a numb state knows that what is happening at that moment is a normal neurological function designed to protect him or her. That person is not crazy or bad or different; his or her brain and ANS are simply responding to a real or perceived threat.

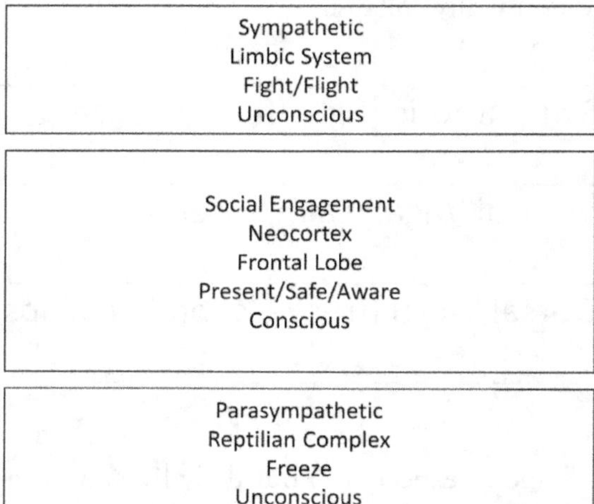

TINSA uses the foundation so that people can see

1. how they function;
2. their daily state of emotional arousal and regulation;
3. how their foundation was affected by ADEs;
4. how they have been using unhealthy self-regulatory reactions to control their foundation; and
5. what to do in healthy ways that can help them regulate their own systems without the use of unhealthy self-regulation or addiction.

Now that we have seen how TINSA uses the concept of a foundation to explain the various parts and functions of our autonomic nervous system, we can use it to demonstrate which part of the triune brain is correlated with the three responses of the autonomic nervous system.

Similar to Porges's polyvagal explanation of our autonomic nervous system, MacLean uses a three-section explanation to show us how the human brain formed, each part's function, and how we can interrelate to others. Using the foundation of regulation, we can decipher what is happening inside our brains, bringing our unconscious reactions to our conscious minds, which enables us to better control and regulate our emotions and our reactions.

It is tempting to equate the three different brain formations discovered by MacLean to the three branches of our autonomic nervous system, although this hypothesis is mine alone and has not yet been shared with the scientific community. However, we can associate the frontal lobe with the ventral vagal nerve. Here the ventral vagal, when functioning properly, keeps the sympathetic nerve in check, reduces cardiac output, and slows down our breathing, leaving us with a clear perception of safety and calm. The other two brains, the mammalian and reptilian, do not have such a direct correlation to MacLean's theory.

However, we can make an argument that when there is a large enough threat, our autonomic nervous system (automatic) will take charge, effectively shutting off most activity to our frontal lobe, thus hijacking the normal function as a defensive posture. During a threat, first our sympathetic nerve will respond, taking us into fight and flight. If this system is successful, our ventral vagal can return to normal functioning. But if the sympathetic fails in eliminating the threat, the dorsal vagal will activate as a fail-safe system and send the individual into a state of freeze, immobilization, and finally total shutdown. Porges notes that freeze occurs when the fight or flight and the dorsal vagal come on at the same time. And finally, if all else fails, the individual will go into full dorsal vagal shutdown, leaving him or her to submit, become immobilized, and ultimately collapse (faint or pass out).

In an attempt to clarify and give more understanding to how the brain and nervous system work together, it is important to note that anytime the threat is large enough, our two older brains take over. This is what we term *hijack* because this response is out of our conscious control. It is also important to remember that when the brain is hijacked in this way, the majority of the frontal lobe turns off out of necessity, and we react rather than respond *without* conscious thought. Our ability to make good decisions, weigh consequences, or consider others is virtually nonexistent. This can go a long way in answering the question as to why addicts seem to lack the ability to see that what they are about to do could harm them, their relationship, career, freedom, family, or even their life. Threats, real or imagined, can trigger the brain into an automatic reaction, turning off the frontal lobe and causing the individual to react to the threat unconsciously with the unconscious brains.

Our limbic and reptilian brains are reactive mechanisms and do not possess the ability to consciously respond. This reaction is automatic and not within our conscious ability to control without

1. a conscious awareness of the reactions; and
2. a practiced ability to assist the frontal lobe to reengage.

With their automatic reactions, many of my clients have found themselves ruining relationships, careers, reputations, and even their personal freedom. Trapped in the unconscious brain's automatic response, addicts lack the awareness and capacity to think things through. The brain works in one way, and when triggered, it automatically switches into a defensive posture out of self-protection.

To further simplify, TINSA provides this knowledge to patients so they can see how their autonomic nervous systems are affected and responding *normally* to a threat. The goal then is to help the client to determine if the threat is real or an automatic response that is attempting to block off the feelings, sensations, or beliefs that are now triggered by earlier, unresolved wounds.

Knowing the Foundation

When we utilize the foundation to describe how our brains and autonomic nervous systems react or respond to events, we use words that describe feelings and sensations to know which system is currently active. Beginning with our desired state of life, we explain what life is like when we are operating primarily from our frontal lobe and our ventral vagal nerve is operating optimally. We all wish to feel peaceful and calm as well as present and aware. We wish to get along with others and have a sense of connection and belonging. When "in our foundation," we feel warm, open, calm, receptive, connected, engaged, present, happy, hopeful, expansive, tender, confident, powerful, safe, trusting, optimistic, positive, creative, playful, and valuable. We possess the ability to socially engage and form intimate bonds with those we love.

The frontal lobe is the key to our regulation and to these attributes, for only here do we have any real conscious ability to change our reactions through conscious choice, reason, problem solving, impulse control, and spontaneity. Our frontal lobe makes us human, allowing us to bargain with our instincts instead of automatically acting on them.

In TINSA we are quick to point out that sex addiction may be an indicator that our frontal lobe or social engagement system is offline or severely skewed. The resultant cascade effect disables our ability to really know safety, so we are unable to experience authenticity or vulnerability, both of which are requirements for deep intimacy and bonding. Later we will describe what occurs with the frontal lobe when ADEs have affected this region.

Next, we describe a sympathetic or limbic response to an event by stating that we have left our foundation; we have left the frontal lobe of calm and logic. We leave the foundation after a real or perceived threat. Most of us have had the experience of being cut off in traffic. When a sudden threat emerges, our bodies react through adrenaline, tension, sharpened focus, and increased heart rate. We feel angry, threatened, offended, hurt, scared, or terrified, depending on the size of the threat. Living sympathetically produces feelings and sensations of fear, anger, judgment, ridicule, anxiety, and paranoia. We can be shaky, obsessive, impulsive, panicked, insecure, hostile, or critical. As we shall see, living in this state can also be a by-product of having experienced ADEs that have changed the way our brains and nervous systems form and react to threats, real or perceived.

Finally, clients learn to recognize when they have gone out of their foundation and are having a dorsal vagal reaction. A dorsal vagal reaction can occur when something is truly life threatening, such as a severe car crash, the sudden loss of a loved one, being robbed at gunpoint, being raped, or discovering the person you trust the most has betrayed you through some form of infidelity. Usually, however, clients show the dorsal response when neither fighting nor escaping is an option. Many rape or sexual abuse victims describe this occurring when they were forced to submit, were rendered helpless and powerless, or could not escape the threat. We see many partners in this frozen, numb space when their discovery of the client's addiction is still fresh. Their worlds have been shattered, dreams imploded, and complete shutdown appears to be the only method of response and self-protection from the knowledge that their partner is addicted to sex. We know we are in this state when we feel cold, numb, dizzy, frozen, hollow, disconnected, spacey, heavy, nauseous, queasy, stuck, hopeless, helpless, blocked, confused, or entirely submissive.

It is incredibly important to note that anytime we are out of our foundation, either through our sympathetic reaction or through our dorsal reaction, we are *dissociated*. TINSA describes this state of dissociation as the complete loss of conscious choice. When dissociated, the client has lost all healthy, functional, thought-out coping mechanisms. When the unconscious brains activate to protect us from threat, the frontal lobe disengages as a further measure to ensure safety. When we see a tiger, we don't need to decide if it is dangerous or take the time to count its stripes—we run! We are in a state of hijack, left to the lower brain's reactions and responses for safety.

ADEs and the Foundation of Regulation

As described earlier, ADEs come in all shapes and sizes. Most of the trauma we see is not from a single event but from repeated events happening or not happening that cause the brain and nervous system to lose the optimal ability to function socially. The trauma caused through ADEs is subjective, meaning that what is traumatic to one person may not be traumatic to another. However, those who have experienced the events that were outlined earlier in this book will demonstrate a marked inability to stay within their frontal lobes (within their foundations) and therefore are subjected to living life either in a sympathetic state (fight or flight) or in a dorsal state (frozen, numb, out of touch). But why? How do these ADEs play such a crucial role in how our brain and nervous systems operate?

By using the foundation, TINSA teaches clients how these adverse experiences have affected normal functioning by actually shrinking the capacity for the frontal lobe to respond. Therefore, we point out that unresolved ADEs have actually shrunk our foundation and our ability to respond with true awareness. In essence, the person with unresolved ADEs is predisposed to a sympathetic or dorsal response.

An adverse experience that is too large for the individual to process with the frontal lobe will stay unresolved in the person's visual and body memories. Each overwhelming event then shrinks the capacity for a frontal lobe response to deal with the threat. Once formed, every other event that is remotely similar will reengage the initial response and cause the individual to use the same method to extinguish the threat with fight, flight, or freeze.

We have also found that the earlier the event, the more established the freeze response. Infants and toddlers, incapable of any defense that would require escaping or fighting, will utilize the only line of defense possible: shutdown, immobilization, and eventual collapse.

Other Effects of the Foundation of Regulation

Most addicts that we treat have also undergone another form of ADE that is mostly unintentional and severely underrecognized. The symptoms of these ADEs are seen in a profound inability to sense, know, regulate, or express their emotions. Addicts appear to struggle with their emotional environment regardless of the type of addiction, but it is especially evident in sex addicts and the underlying intimacy disorder. We must have feelings to be vulnerable, and we must be able to know, regulate, and express our feelings and experience.

Emotional Vacancy

Infants and young children are by nature unregulated. When born, we are a ball of instinctual demands that must be met to ensure our physical survival. What separates us from other mammals, however, is that the sensations and emotions that express these instincts must be tended to, groomed, and practiced if we are to develop healthy emotional lives. TINSA uses the idea of scaffolding. Here we teach that the infant and toddler must be supported by a stronger nervous system in order for the nervous system to mature into a healthy, self-sufficient system capable of awareness of an emotion, understanding of the emotion, regulation of the emotion, and a socially acceptable expression of the emotion. Most of the clients we see come from households where healthy emotional expression was absent. We may have received all the material things we needed for health, but when it came to emotions, they either were not allowed; were controlled, shamed, ridiculed; or were used as a way to manipulate our behaviors.

When I was growing up in my parents' household, feelings and emotions were not allowed. If I tried to express my concerns vocally, those concerns were either met with disapproval or discounted altogether. If I then got upset or angry, those emotions were met with even more disapproval and discipline. The more I fought against my parents' lack of emotional nurturing, the more resistance I would get back, and so I quickly came to understand that there was no way to either talk my way or fight my way out of these problems.

The only way to survive in that household was to submit, which caused me to live in a state of dissociation. I could either try to find connection or choose to survive, and I chose to survive every time. During these instances of adverse developmental experiences, at an age when my defenses were limited, I learned that it was best to give up, dissociate, and keep everything in. I learned to give up my authenticity and become what others wanted me to be.

For me and many clients we treat, we see that continuing to use dissociative responses to threats became a way of life all throughout childhood and into adulthood. Many clients start treatment with no idea how to even access their emotions, let alone regulate or express them. They learned to regulate their systems by avoiding emotions through unhealthy self-regulation. When our beginnings start with the absence of emotional support, we quickly learn ways to become our own support.

Triggers

TINSA defines triggers as any person, place, event, or bodily sensation or memory that elicits an automatic defensive response. People with ADEs, because of their reduced ability to stay within their frontal lobes, are hyperfocused to threat. As mentioned earlier, the threat can be real (someone shouting at you) or perceived (a facial expression perceived as conveying disapproval). The greater the unresolved ADEs, the greater the number of triggers. As mentioned earlier, there is an infinitely small amount of overlap required between a current event and a previous painful experience to set off our sympathetic or dorsal responses. An example most sex addicts and their partners often experience has to do with a simple cell phone. Before discovery, a cell phone may be just a cell phone, but after discovery, the very sight or sound of the cell phone can bring the betrayed partner back to square one, overwhelmed with pain, fear, and betrayal. It is the same with all of our unresolved ADEs that have accumulated throughout our lifetime. Early experiences of rejection or neglect can shape our future lives, unconsciously guiding us to avoid the possibility of these events at all costs.

In the next chapter, we describe how TINSA explains the predisposition to addictions as an innocent means of self-protection. ADEs have affected our brain and autonomic nervous systems so that the only way we could find any calm in our turbulent emotional systems was to do it ourselves.

Six

HOW SELF-REGULATION BEHAVIORS

LEAD TO ADDICTION

Michael Barta Ph.D., LPC, CSAT-S

The neurobiological changes that occur within a child who experiences trauma can cause that child's reality to become distorted, thereby limiting the capacity for human intimacy. Lack of attunement in infancy can lead to an inability to form adult connections. Ultimately this can lead a person to use potentially addictive behaviors or substances as coping mechanisms and neurological regulatory devices. Once hooked on the biochemicals that these regulatory behaviors and substances provide, what was once solely an issue of unresolved traumatic experience now becomes a much bigger problem of addiction. The pathway to healing and recovery begins with the addict's ability to recognize that there is a difference between reality and what our minds falsely perceive as reality due to unresolved trauma and the damage it has inflicted on our neurological systems.

Attunement grooms a child's nervous system to function self-sufficiently through nonverbal communication. Correct attunement occurs when we are able to communicate nonverbally with our caregivers in such a way that they communicate back to us and meet our emotional needs, such as when a mother soothes a crying baby. This two-way exchange builds our capacity for empathy and our ability to engage socially. When a child does not receive proper attunement, his or her ability to read nonverbal social cues and socially engage is severely limited. It becomes more natural for that person to withdraw from human connection, and it is nearly impossible for him or her to successfully bond with others in an authentic way.

Equally damaging are the other adverse developmental experiences mentioned earlier in the book, including people or events that did not allow adequate protection or connection and a system that was devoid of emotions.

Adverse developmental experiences are stored as trauma in a child, causing a propensity for triggers and narrowing the foundation of regulation. When this happens, our brain is hijacked, and we react from our more primitive responses. Depending on the amount of stored trauma and associated triggers we have, this hijacking can become constant, trapping us in states of overactive sympathetic response or overactive dorsal vagal response. Instead of responding to everyday life from our social engagement system, we live constantly in a dissociated state, overreacting with a fight-or-flight reflex or stuck with an inability to respond at all as we freeze in place. None of this is our fault. Our systems were rewired from early on to survive through these primitive responses because we never received the support we needed to fully develop neurologically.

Living with the long-term effects of unresolved trauma is a painful existence. Living in states of dissociation, whether in sympathetic or in dorsal reactivity, can be harrowing and excruciating, and to cope we adapt what TINSA calls *regulatory behaviors* from a very young age. These behaviors can come in many forms. Most start out rather benignly in an attempt to regulate the self: isolating behaviors, fantasy, food, and even sexual arousal. We partake in these behaviors in an effort to manage the pain of dissociation. As traumatized individuals, we use regulatory behaviors in an attempt to get back into the calming confines of our foundation. Quite simply, regulatory behaviors are used as a way to self-regulate our ineffective nervous systems.

Traumatized individuals adapt self-regulation from a very young age just so that they can feel normal. Unfortunately many of these behaviors, usually stumbled upon by accident, can affect the brain in ways that will become addictive. Sexual fantasy, masturbation, pornography, or early sexual experiences with others can and do produce large amounts of dopamine. When they are used repeatedly to regulate mood, the brain will employ the process of downregulation, further removing dopamine receptors to regulate the amount received. The brain can't stop you from bombarding it with dopamine, but it can control how much it will allow in. Once this process happens, the individual will need to escalate the behavior in order to get enough dopamine since the brain has shut down receptors. Now they are hooked. A behavior that once produced a high is now needed simply to avoid the pain of not having enough. We call this withdrawal.

Many people who have used regulatory behaviors to cope with adverse developmental experiences remember the first time they did so. I have a client who stated that he clearly remembered being five years old, thumbing through a lingerie catalog, and coming upon the bra section. While most little boys and little girls will find these kinds of things funny or fascinating, this little boy noticed a huge change in the feelings that he had within his body and within his mind. Today, at fifty-five years old, this client can still remember this event as if it were yesterday because of the tremendous impact it had on him. When he was looking at these images, he felt good. He felt different than he was normally feeling, and, as he remembers back, he felt that he had somehow escaped both the oppression and the high intensity of his family's household. His brain then recorded this event as a way to escape his emotional pain. He registered the event as a way to temporarily escape from the dissociated states in which he so often found himself.

Without knowing it, what my client was discovering for the first time was an avenue through which he could self-regulate his nervous system. He had finally found a way that he could stop the pain associated with dysregulation, giving him the feeling that everything was okay. Although the feeling was only temporary, his brain recorded that event as a tool that he could use to achieve the same feeling later on if needed. A few years later, in adolescence, he found sexual fantasy and masturbation, just as everyone does, but for him these sexual activities gave him more than just simple pleasure. He had found a way to control his chronic feelings of anxiety and depression and came to rely on them as his only source of self-regulation. For my client, this is how sexual activity became a reliable way to cope. Many people who suffer from sex addiction share very similar accounts.

The many different behaviors used by people to regulate only get more expansive as we get older, sometimes even spilling over into using addictive substances as well. Drinking, drugs, sex, food, and gambling are all forms of regulatory behaviors that can be adapted unconsciously as a means of escaping the feelings that are associated with the pain of having a narrow foundation. When a person is sent into a sympathetic or dorsal state as a result of unresolved past trauma, he or she will drink, eat, use drugs, or engage in sexual fantasy or activity in order to calm and lower the sympathetic charge, which is signaling that a fight-or-flight response is needed. By the same token, if that person finds him- or herself in a dorsal state, he or she will use one or more of those same behaviors to raise the sympathetic charge and escape the depressed and lethargic feelings. What usually happens is that over time, a person will use a cocktail of multiple regulatory behaviors to self-regulate. However, as mentioned, since sex is often the first survival behavior we find, it often remains a person's most reliant tool for self-regulation well into adulthood.

When it comes to the behaviors that people use to regulate, it is important to acknowledge that they are all unconscious behaviors. We don't actually have conscious control over them, even though it may appear that we do. We may use them for mood-altering coping mechanisms, but we do so as a triggered response, meaning that we are at that point operating out of our more primitive neurological systems and not from conscious thought. Beginning when we are very young, self-regulation is nothing more than a coping mechanism that helps people deal with the pain caused by wounds to their vulnerability and authenticity. These behaviors occur from within us out of necessity and automatically as a survival tactic. In fact, adapting and continually partaking in regulatory behaviors is just as automatic as states of dissociation, both of which are natural responses and methods of dealing with the pain of current or past wounds to vulnerability.

Adverse developmental experiences negatively affected our brain and nervous systems, causing us to live not primarily in our social engagement system but in our unconscious systems. What this means is that our emotional brain is really running the show most of the time. While our thinking brain is meant to keep our nervous system in balance, without conscious thought we become prone to living in hyper- or hypo-aroused states, acting instinctively. Under these conditions any reaction we have and any behaviors we use to cope are unconscious, although purposeful, and meant only for survival.

Remember that when we talk about regulation in these contexts, we are talking about overcoming perceived threats to one's life, thus maintaining control and balance of one's own nervous system. For those with stored trauma, misreading sensory stimuli is also an unconscious act. Stored trauma can cause a person to relate current sensory input to past trauma, confusing current circumstances with those past traumatic events. This is all done from the unconscious brain where that trauma is stored. In his book *The Body Keeps the Score*, Van der Kolk writes,

> Ideally our stress hormone system should provide a lightning-fast response to threat, but then quickly return us to equilibrium. In PTSD patients, however, the stress hormone system fails at this balancing act. Fight/flight/freeze signals continue after the danger is over and… do not return to normal. Instead, the continued secretion of stress hormones is expressed as agitation and panic and, in the long term, wreaks havoc with their health. (2014, 30)

To outsiders, sexual acting out as a form of self-regulation in adulthood may seem like an unnecessary response or overreaction to everyday difficulties, but it is an unconscious response. Remember, when things occur in the present that trigger or remind us of these past wounds, we are sent outside of our foundation and are not acting in line with what is actually occurring. Gabor Maté (2010) explains that implicit memory causes us to react to something in the present as a result of something that happened in the past. We do not realize what is happening at the time, but we are not reacting to what is happening right now; the hurt causing this reaction was inflicted in the past.

When traumatized individuals are triggered by implicit memory, they are, without their own conscious consent, cast out of their foundation and into dissociated states where they are likely to act out as a means of regulation. Under these circumstances they will do just about anything, sometimes partaking in a broad range of behaviors in order to get back to their foundation. What most commonly occurs, though, is that traumatized individuals will use the very same regulatory behavior or behaviors that are most familiar or that were used to cope with the original trauma. In other words, our first solution and method of self-regulation is usually the one that we're going to keep coming back to. And because sexual pleasure is such a developmental occurrence, it is often the first thing we find as a self-regulating tool and can therefore remain our primary regulatory behavior for the rest of our lives.

Another contributor to the unconscious state of being in which we find ourselves while acting out is that the chronic stress of the original adverse developmental experiences induces desensitization. When as children we experience repetitive trauma, our body's natural stress response becomes overwhelmed, causing it in some cases to malfunction, and propelling a person to "numb out." This response continues to occur automatically into adulthood whenever we are reminded of past trauma or when we are plagued by stressful circumstances in general.

When under stress, traumatized individuals do not have the capacity to handle the situation in the same way that the average person does. Anytime we are triggered and sent outside of our foundation, not only are we operating out of our unconscious brain, but we are actually in a state of dissociation. Therefore, acting out under these conditions not only lacks rational, conscious thought but also lacks the proper neurological functioning necessary for emotional awareness. In response to the conditional traumatic stimuli that can be perceived in everyday experiences, traumatized individuals tend to numb out behaviorally and mentally. It is this combination of irrational thought and dissociation that causes traumatized individuals to lack concern for the possible consequences of their actions when they are employing their regulatory behaviors.

In addition to using regulatory behaviors to decrease sympathetic-charge fight or flight and to decrease dorsal reaction, immobilize, and numb, people will use sexually compulsive behavior to re-create an earlier trauma state. Reenactment, the process of repeating something traumatic over and over with the intent that it will eventually result in a different outcome, is another way in which people cope with trauma, partaking chronically in particular regulatory behaviors in an attempt to repeat an early wounding event. Done without conscious awareness, reenactment involves the compulsion to repeat the actions that caused the problem in the first place. As people who suffer from the effects of adverse developmental experiences, we are inextricably drawn into situations that replicate the original trauma in both obvious and less obvious ways, and we are often compelled to reenact our early traumas in our daily lives. What we are trying to do is re-create or establish a new norm that is different from the original trauma, and so we will repeat the trauma over and over, trying to get it to work out. Doing so gives us the illusion that we now have power over an event in which we were once powerless. The original trauma could have occurred in many forms, such as sexual abuse, deeply shaming experiences, or being rejected, neglected, or abandoned, but reenactment could also just be an effort to complete emotionally vacant experiences such as a lack of attunement or a lack of intimacy from our caregivers.

Reenactment, though, comes with serious repercussions. Not only does it fail to resolve the original trauma, but it can also strengthen the intensity of the traumatic memory or memories, sending us into a vicious cycle of recalling trauma and dissociation. "It is likely that the frequent re-living of a traumatic event in flashbacks or nightmares causes a re-release of stress hormones which further kindle the strength of the memory trace," writes Van der Kolk. "Such a positive feedback loop could cause subclinical PTSD to escalate into clinical PTSD, in which the strength of the memories seem so deeply engraved that Pitman and Orr have called it 'the Black Hole' in the mental life of the PTSD patient, that attracts all associations to it, and saps current life of its significance" (1994, 260).

As discussed, a vast array of regulatory behaviors can be used to cope with the effects of adverse developmental experiences, but specifically, sex is often used as a reenactment tool because sex is linked to the very same emotional components within us that have been wounded: our vulnerability and our authenticity. By nature, we are meant to connect deeply and intimately with others. However, when that instinctual response is not equally met, it is stored as trauma in the body, and it incurs damage to our ability to be vulnerable and authentic. Developmentally wounded people tend to act out sexually and choose sex as a regulatory behavior as they try to achieve a different outcome to these early incomplete instinctual responses to connect. This never works, however, because intimacy is not possible while a person is operating in states of dissociation.

Finally, according to Patrick Weeg, a clinical social worker in Denver, Colorado, there is another reason for regulatory behaviors:

It should also be mentioned that sometimes those behaviors and substances are actually used as a means of staying outside the foundation on purpose. This has been associated with the need to feel more safety. For example, someone who was in a very dangerous situation all throughout childhood might actually feel more comfortable living

in a hyper-aroused state because then they can see any danger coming and feel powerful as well to protect themselves—something they couldn't feel before (therefore they use cocaine, amphetamines, risk taking, reenactments, etc.).
On the flip side, people often want to stay in a shut-down, hypo-aroused state to prevent themselves from feeling the pain or rage or overwhelming emotions and sensations, so they keep themselves in a shut-down state. The classic example is Vietnam vets using opioids when they were in Vietnam and when they came home to prevent themselves from remembering or experiencing the painful emotions and sensations that went with memory. (personal communication)

Unfortunately, these people cannot live in a state of calm.

The bottom line is this: for those of us who suffer from the effects of past trauma, all regulatory behaviors are unconscious efforts to feel normal and to get us back into our foundation. They have one purpose: to kill pain. Our brains and nervous systems don't work the same way as those of a person who received healthy attunement. We are molded to react instinctively to everyday occurrences from our unconscious regulatory responses due to an abundant amount of stored trauma within our hippocampus. Yet we make up so many fallacies about ourselves, including that we are bad people, and we judge ourselves so harshly. We carry shame and guilt for acts that are purely a natural biological response to our environment.

Sex addiction at its core is an intimacy disorder. As traumatized individuals, our natural ability to be vulnerable and authentic and therefore intimate with others has been extinguished either by our failed attempts to express those same sentiments from a young age with our caregivers or through other similar adverse developmental experiences. Furthermore, these events stifle the development of our brains and nervous systems; as a result, we have difficulty operating out of our frontal lobes and staying within the calm confines of our foundation of regulation.

We are unable to self-regulate and easily become hijacked by our sympathetic or dorsal reaction. To cope, we resort to self-regulation using regulatory behaviors, many of which—like sex and food—are actually essential to both our individual survival and to the survival of our species. Because of this, the brain is programmed to encourage participation in these activities, and it does so by triggering the dopamine response in the rewards center of the brain, resulting in feelings of pleasure. The problem this causes is that we can become biochemically addicted to this rush. In fact, to demonstrate just how addictive regulatory behaviors can be, Robert Weiss writes that "addictive substances and addictive behaviors trigger the same basic neurochemical pleasure response—primarily the release of dopamine (pleasure) along with adrenaline (excitement) and oxytocin (love and connection), serotonin (emotional well-being) and a variety of endorphins (euphoria) resulting in feelings of pleasure, excitement, and most important, distraction and emotional escape" (2015a., 4).

While many people believe that behavioral addictions, including sex addiction, are simply bad habits formed over time, these addictions are in fact deeply biological. When sex is used as a self-regulating tool early in life, be it through exposure to online porn, masturbation, fantasy, or exposure to anything that is sexual in nature, it floods the synapses with pleasure-producing neurochemicals. For those with adverse developmental experiences and who therefore have a deficit of dopamine receptors, the brain will register at that point that it finally, for at least this moment in time, feels normal. This is not to be confused with the feeling of ecstasy or of being on a high. Rather, it simply gives the individual a sense of peace and calm. It is the feeling of finally getting enough dopamine. Once registered, this event is adapted into automatic behaviors, and we keep coming back to it to feel good and as a continual means of coping with neurological irregularities. Without realizing it, from a very young age we are using sexual arousal to manage our life. We are using it to regulate our emotions. And because sex is often one of our earliest regulatory behaviors, we find it can also be one of our most long-lasting addictions. Ironically, after chronic use of sex as a regulatory behavior, downregulation begins to occur, leaving us with the need for more and more dopamine through higher-risk sexual activity. This is precisely how sexual arousal becomes an addiction.

Reenactment can also become addicting. Just as when we use regulatory behaviors to cope, while we are repeating past trauma, we are simultaneously becoming hooked on our own neurochemicals. "When people relive the trauma, they recreate a similar neurochemical state that occurred at the time of the trauma, the release of adrenaline and endorphins," states Peter Levine. "Now, adrenaline is addictive, it is like getting a speed high. And they get addicted not only to the adrenaline but to the endorphins; it's like having a drug cocktail of amphetamines and morphine" (2010). Not only can repeating the trauma become addictive in this way, getting a person hooked on the neurotransmitters that are released each time, but so too can talk therapies become addicting for a person with past trauma, because each time they try to talk out their past trauma, the same stimulating and addicting neurotransmitters are released, just as they were during the original event.

TINSA defines sex addiction as a tool used by traumatized individuals to get back into their foundation of regulation. It is part of our automatic response system, primarily an emotional brain process. The frontal lobe is disengaged during one's involvement in the addictive cycle and when engaged in the addictive behaviors, and so addiction is merely a result of misinterpreted threats to our ability to regulate. At the core of addiction is the unconscious need to rid ourselves of pain. Sexual activity and thought processes such as objectification, manipulation, and the constant pursuit of sexual opportunity or sexual release are all just forms of constant, unconscious self-regulation. And while sexual acting out and other regulation can get a person back into his foundation, it does so only temporarily, because the true catalyst for and root cause of the dissociated states, the unresolved traumas, have not properly been addressed and resolved. Unfortunately, at this point in the addictive cycle, it does not matter much to an addict if his behaviors are only working temporarily, because by this time he is hooked. A combination of the constant neurological discomfort and the awful feelings of neurochemical withdrawal from dopamine depletion keeps us engaging in the behaviors time and time again.

Sex addiction is all about control. It is about unconsciously controlling your emotions in an attempt to increase, mitigate, or reduce increased sympathetic or dorsal response. "All addictions—whether to drugs or to non-drug behaviors—share the same brain circuits and brain chemicals," writes Maté.

"On the biochemical level the purpose of all addictions is to create an altered physiological state in the brain" (2010, 137).

Once a person becomes addicted to sex, the repercussions it can have on the psyche are immense. Patrick Carnes summarized the four core beliefs that sex addicts have about themselves in his book *Out of the Shadows*:

1. I am basically a bad/unworthy person.
2. No one would love me as I am, or if you really knew me, you would reject me.
3. My needs are never going to be met if I have to depend upon others.
4. Sex is my most important need. (2001, 152)

The first three of these core beliefs reflect how incredibly isolating and lonely sex addiction is. As discussed in chapter 5, unresolved early trauma results in insecure systems that carry over into adulthood and limit our ability to fully connect with others. It is these insecure systems that obstruct our capacity for vulnerability, authenticity, and true intimacy, making sex addiction quite lonesome. When we then seek out sexual activity that is harmful to ourselves or others in an attempt to change the experience of the pain associated with these limitations, we feel even more isolated. Number 4 of these core beliefs, "sex is my most important need," reflects just how absolutely necessary sex becomes to the addict as a means of temporary emotional stability and of escaping pain. The sad reality of sex addiction is that the need for the addictive behavior itself is put above and before everything else in the addict's life without any conscious consent.

Another unfortunate consequence of sexual addiction is that it can cause us to become emotionally vacant in almost every area of our life, prohibiting us from feeling joyful emotions. Continual avoidance of vulnerability can make us numb to any feeling whatsoever, whether it is before, during, or after our sexual acting out. When we attempt to use sex or other addictive actions or substances to awaken these dulled feelings, it is only a temporary fix. "The addict's reliance on the drug to reawaken his dulled feelings is no adolescent caprice," writes Maté. "The dullness is itself a consequence of an emotional malfunction not of the addict's making; the internal shutdown of vulnerabil-ity" (2010, 40). Unless the root problem of addiction is addressed, this vicious cycle will continue, and the individual's capability to harbor joyful emotions will never manifest.

While avoiding vulnerability may be the best way for a child to survive in an emotionally vacant home, it can wreak havoc on a person's happiness and well-being as an adult when the escape route becomes automatic. "The automatic repression of painful emotion is a helpless child's prime defense mechanism and can enable the child to endure trauma that would otherwise be catastrophic," writes Maté. "The unfortunate consequence is a wholesale dulling of emotional awareness" (2008, 40). In other words, we do not get to pick and choose which emotions we can suppress. When the wall of repression goes up, it keeps out the joy along with the sadness, the calm as well as the chaos. Although it may be true that engaging in regulatory behaviors served a real purpose in our childhood when we were faced with adverse develop-mental experiences and a lack of attunement, in the end we become reliant on and addicted to these behaviors that rob us of the capacity to experience true happiness.

In addition to an inability to have a sense of control, a sense of belonging, the capacity to express authenticity, to be authentic, and to be intimate with another individual, sex addiction can have a vast amount of negative repercus-sions for a person's life. As discussed in chapter 1, the loss of jobs, relation-ships, and reputations can be attributed to sex and pornography addictions. In the media we have seen many examples of this with high-profile figures risking all of these very same things in order to keep engaging in their sexual acting out. The recent exposure of sexual impropriety by actors, comedians, pro-ducers, and political leaders points to the out-of-control sexual nature of the addict, and the depth and magnitude of this very real phenomenon. Sexual addiction has caused many of these men to cross boundaries that they never would have crossed if their frontal lobes were engaged and they were conscious of the possible consequences. I am not trying to indicate at all that these men are not fully responsible for their actions, and I do not want to label all as mere sex addicts. There is a large difference between the sexual addict and the sexual predator who forces his sexual will on others. Of course, there is only one explanation for this: sex addicts have an absolute dependence on sex for self-regulation. Decisions that we make as traumatized individuals are not coming from the prefrontal areas of our brains. Stored triggers that exist from past trauma result in a hijacking of the brain, which makes conscious, rational thoughts impossible. Under these circumstances, we cannot possibly think rationally enough to be concerned with repercussions. Unfortunately, the consequential biochemical release from regulatory behavior can drive the addiction to a point where the repercussions could be catastrophic. "Decisions that we may believe to be freely made can arise from unconscious emotional drives or subliminal beliefs," writes Maté. "They can be dictated by brain mechanisms programmed early in childhood and determined by events of which we have no recollections. The stronger a person's automatic brain mechanisms and the weaker the parts of the brain that can impose conscious control, the less true freedom that person will be able to exercise in her life" (2010, 303).

Not only do we engage in our addictions unconsciously and therefore without regard for possible repercussions, but once we're addicted we also operate in a vicious cycle where engaging in the addictive behavior only promotes further engagement. In 1983 Patrick Carnes introduced this self-repeating cycle of sexual addiction. Since that time, the cycle has been modified many times, giving us more insight into the cycle of addiction.

The following addiction cycle that TINSA uses was adapted with permission from Dr. Robert Warren and Steven DeLugach, MS, LPC, CSAT-S, two colleagues who specialize in the treatment of sexual addiction. For the sex addict, it is important to know just what is happening neurologically, biologically, and behaviorally. Once aware, the addict has a much better chance to leave the cycle before any real harm can be done.

ADDICTION CYCLE

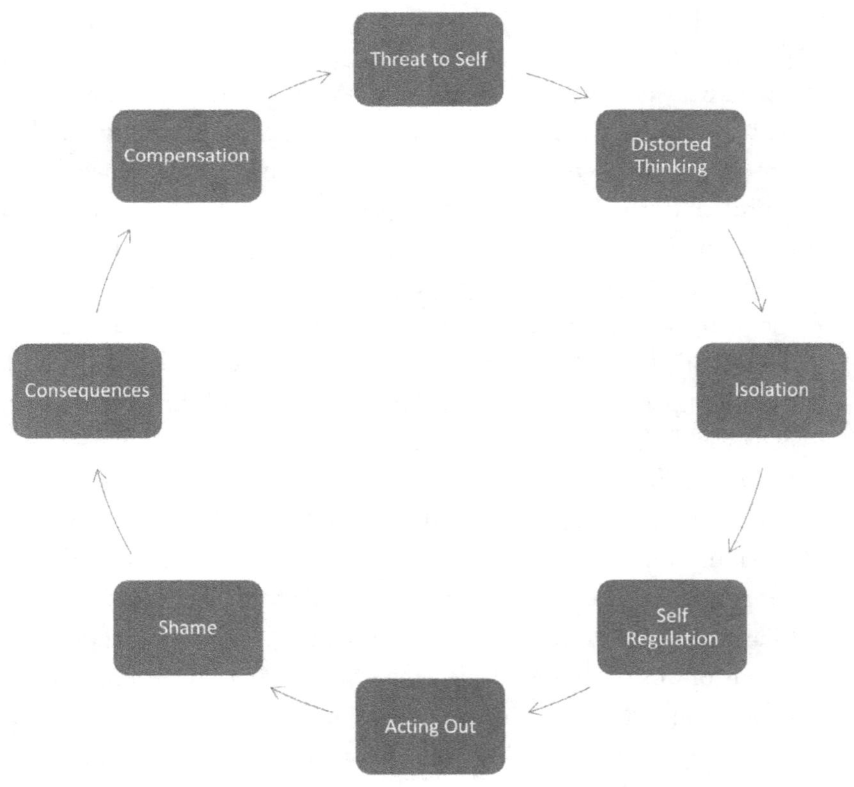

Adapted from Steven DeLugach, MS, LPC and Robert Warren, PhD's model of the Addiction Cycle. Used with permission. All rights reserved.

1. Threats to self: TINSA labels any threat to the self that is either real or imagined as the starting point of the addictive cycle. These are our triggers. Threats can be in the form of people, places, events, sensations, feelings, thoughts, smells, and sounds. Most often triggers are some sort of "pain agent." Pain agents include both emotional/psychological and physical discomfort, either from short-term or long-term experiences. Depression, anxiety, loneliness, boredom, stress, shame, anger, and any other uncomfortable feeling can easily trigger a sex addict's desire to escape or avoid. A trigger then activates our defense system and depending on the size, will employ our sympathetic system or dorsal systems. Remember, once triggered, we have left the foundation, the frontal lobe disengages, and we are left at the mercy of our unconscious brain and how it will automatically respond to a threat, whether real or imagined. What is important to note here is that professionals in the therapeutic community have stated that once started on the addictive cycle, the neurochemicals begin to produce the feelings associated with the high, so the high of the addiction happens well before the actual sexual act.

2. Distorted thinking: Distorted thoughts occur when we are reacting unconsciously. Triggers cause the person to "make things up." Here previous wounds are brought back to life and appear as if they are happening in the present moment. The unconscious limbic and reptilian brains do not think; they simply react, and their reaction takes us out of our frontal lobe, and the nonthinking but reacting unconscious brain engages. This brain reminds us just how poorly we are treated, or how unjust it is that we work so hard and our partner denies us sex. We can also hear that we deserve to unwind, that our actions aren't hurting anyone, or that all men do it. Our thoughts become dissociated from our thinking brain, and these thoughts bring on all justification and rationalization. Again, the unconscious brain ignores all possibility of consequence. Our distorted thought comes in to justify our regulatory behaviors. We begin to close down and return to our self-regulation.

3. Isolation: Once dissociated, we go back to our old methods of dissolving or minimizing threat. Since our original trauma happened, isolation was our unconscious solace. When others are not there to help regulate our systems, we put our walls up and "take care of ourselves." Self-regulation can be traced back to very early ages, for in most cases of ADEs there was no one to rely upon but the self. "I got this" is the famous call of the sex addict; after all, the addict has been managing his or her own emotions from an early age. We isolate and turn inward, seemingly uncoupling and extinguishing the threat. We feel we cannot be hurt if we do it on our own, so once again we attempt to take control and do it on our own.

4. Self-regulation/regulatory behaviors: Self-regulation follows isolation; dealing with our emotions alone proves painful. Addicts find themselves drawn to particular thoughts and behaviors that produce a trancelike state. TINSA postulates that this stage is an attempt to kill pain and to regulate mood for brief periods of time. Our unconscious brains have stored antidotes to pain and provide us with a multitude of ideas in our storehouse of pain-killing remedies. In this trancelike state, the addict finds himself repeating behaviors again and again that have worked in the past. The rituals involved are numerous, from primping and grooming, to cruising favorite websites or streets known for prostitution, to a subtler form of objectification. This stage appears to be where the addict lives most of the time, tantalizing the self, escaping pain, and attempting to emotionally regulate. Whatever form the rituals take, they show that the addict is clearly on the hunt for his fix, and the more he engages in these behaviors, the more dopamine and other neurochemicals engage. The addict is "high" before he acts out.

5. TINSA pays particular attention to the self-regulation stage, because this appears to be where we store our potent techniques to kill pain or avoid pain. Until fully stopped for a certain amount of time, the addict can be said to be "always on." Sex addicts look for opportunity, and the self-regularized state is making sure one is ready when the chance occurs.

6. Sexual acting out: There are as many forms of acting out as there are individuals addicted to sex. Whether it is limited to pornography and masturbation, or with behaviors that include others, legal or illegal, the main goal is the final dose of neurochemical release produced by orgasm. Acting out is never about intimacy or connection; ironically, it is to avoid these things and escape pain. Most addicts I treat say that acting out was never as good as they had anticipated, and they remark that the real high is in the ritual and fantasy of self-regulation. Every sex addict knows the feeling of despair after an addictive orgasm has occurred, for here he is unmercifully slammed back into the frontal lobe, and clear thinking immediately resumes.

7. Shame: Once the acting out is complete, disassociation stops, the frontal lobe comes online, and decision making and self-judgment return. It is here that the addict experiences the shame of what has just occurred. He immediately feels remorse for having failed and hurt himself and his loved ones once again. He will now try to stuff the shame of the behavior, swearing off, checking his tracks to remain undiscovered. Despair, self-loathing, hopelessness, and fear dominate the addict's mind. What most nonaddicts do not realize is that acting out is not the main aim for the addict. The primary goal is to escape as much reality as possible.

8. Consequence: Here both inner and outer consequences occur. Inner consequences consist of mental anguish: the fear of being discovered, paranoia concerning who might know, self-disgust, fear, anxiety, and diminished self-esteem. We purposefully distance ourselves from those we love because of guilt and shame. On the other hand, outer consequences can include actually being exposed or discovered, broken trust, devastated marriages or relationships, public shame and ridicule, arrest, job loss, damaged reputation, and in extreme cases, loss of life.

9. Compensation: There is not an addict reading this book who is not familiar with compensation—our feeble attempts to make right what we have just done, to appease our guilt and shame, and in most cases, throw our partners off our track. These can include love notes, gifts,

flowers, trips, loving texts and phone calls, or more obsessive behaviors such as cleaning the house, doing extra work, or being especially kind for several days.

10. Repeating the cycle: After we compensate, we can feel better for a period of time, but it does not last. Our promises to ourselves and our loved ones soon begin to fade. Once established, the addiction will repeat this cycle endlessly, for each acting-out cycle produces more shame and more need for further escape. Here is a man continually creating more and more threat to himself; he builds more triggers that will then ignite another go-round.

This depiction of the stages of sex addiction mirrors my own experience with sex addiction and the experiences I hear from my clients, beginning with becoming triggered and being sent into a dissociated state. Sex addicts constantly find themselves in a trancelike state that increases dopamine, epinephrine, oxytocin, and other mood-altering brain chemicals. In these trancelike states, they are unable to recognize any significant threat to their personal well-being or to their family, reputation, or employment. Then, once the trancelike state is broken through the completion of their ritual, they experience immediate numbing, followed by shame, guilt, remorse, paranoia, and self-loathing, all of which can trigger a traumatized individual to be sent once again into a dissociated state and down the rabbit hole of repetitive acting-out behaviors.

Perhaps one of the most severe consequences to a person who engages in sexual activity as a means of emotional regulation is that his offspring may also become unable to emotionally regulate in a healthy way. Emotional regulation is a learned process passed down from generation to generation through secure and functioning attachment. If one's previous generation had untreated difficulty with emotional regulation, there exists the likelihood that emotional dysregulation will be passed down to the next generation.

Recovery is about expanding the foundation so that we won't easily be sent into a heightened sympathetic state or fall prey to our automatic immobilized response. When we become aware of how our brains and bodies are reacting to a threat, we gain the choice of no longer unconsciously resorting to using our addictive behaviors to autoregulate. We expand the foundation by dealing with the addict's adverse developmental experiences that have never had the chance to be processed. There are many ways to do this; recovery and true healing is possible through the comprehensive knowledge of one's own past trauma, the understanding of one's own neurological processes, appropriate recovery tools, trauma treatment, and support. In the next chapter, we explain how the TINSA model couples with advancements in new understandings regarding addiction and the brain with a well-developed format for the treatment and long-term recovery of sexual addiction.

Seven

HEALING AND RECOVERY

Michael Barta Ph.D., LPC, CSAT-S

In a 2016 announcement, US Surgeon General Vivek Murthy stated that addiction is a chronic brain disease, not a moral failing. The importance of this statement is on par with that of the US surgeon general's 1964 report on the dire effects of smoking. There is no way to express how impactful this new statement is to the millions of people affected by this affliction. For those who could not face the shame of their own or another's addiction, there is now a new understanding of the basis of sex addiction. That being said, new treatment modalities now need to be implemented to keep up with how addiction is being perceived.

The TINSA model differs significantly from the most common treatment modalities because we explain to each client how he became an addict. We rely heavily on educating our clients about their brains, their nervous systems, and how each of these systems was affected and, as a result, autonomically predisposed to addiction. We have found that in educating clients on how their systems operate, we give them more control over their addictions. No longer is the addiction an outside force that is happening to them; they see how they are unconsciously using their behaviors to control their emotions. My clients state they love having this knowledge and feel a great sense of relief from the shame and embarrassment caused through their dissociated actions. I have seen totally shame-filled people quickly turn to self-compassion and accept total responsibility for their healing. Far more than merely digging through the family history and the probable initiators of the addiction, TINSA explains how the brain and ANS reacted to those initiators. In other words, we explain the *how* as well as the *why* regarding the origins of a client's addiction.

When I joined Alcoholics Anonymous, I was told that my addict self was in there, and he wanted to kill me. In my own recovery, however, I have found that nothing is further from the truth. The addictive part of me was formed to protect me and to keep me alive. It formed to kill pain and allow me to tolerate the intolerable. Unfortunately, when this part of me took on a life of its own, I did almost die, many times, but I just couldn't stop because of the large quantities of substances it now took to produce the same effect that small quantities did at the beginning of my acting out. Addiction, or my attempt to regulate and survive, saved my life. I often disclose to my clients that at age thirteen, I was in so much emotional pain from my lack of bonding and attunement that, had I not found alcohol, I believe I would have been a statistic of suicide.

Healing from addiction is a lifelong process. It is not a one-time, one-way process wherein you are forever cured. There are no shortcuts, no magic pills, no silver bullets. Recovery means recovering for the remainder of your life. Like a rocket leaving Earth's gravity, the first part is always the hardest. We are pulling away from a lifetime of patterns and automatic responses that seem to always be pulling us back, tempting us to give in. The good news is that for most people, the initial stage of recovery does not last long. Withdrawal from sex addiction (our brain's craving for the large quantities of dopamine), which manifests as acute feelings of anxiety, paranoia, minor depression, aches and pains, anger, and irritability, lasts only a short time, averaging two to six weeks. Some clients become deeply discouraged when they hear the news that recovery is a lifelong process. But it is more a way of life than a duty or hardship. With recovery comes the ability to learn vulnerability and the indescribably wonderful feelings of peace that come from an authentic expression of self. Recovery, in a nutshell, is learning to increase our foundation of regulation so that we are not blown about by every wind, real or imagined. Recovery is a lifetime process to obtain peace and live comfortably within our own minds and bodies. We choose healthy ways of regulation instead of being slaves to our hijacked systems.

I have been active in my own recovery for over thirty-one years and have never been bored, never felt obligation, and certainly never felt resentment for "having" to recover. Recovery has afforded me the life I've always wanted—excitement, new relationships, self-compassion, love, and a sense that I am finally able to regulate my turbulent emotions and actually join in with other people. I can now let people in, establish trust, and form true and lasting bonds with people I love. Using the TINSA model in my own recovery has enabled me to deal deeply with the core of what made me need reassurance from drugs, alcohol, sex, and food. With my core difficulties either removed or greatly diminished, my brain doesn't automatically take over to use my old, effective but debilitating survival behaviors. Recovery means returning to the original me before adverse development changed my brain, my nervous system, and my beliefs about myself, relationships, and life. Recovery is wonderful—filled with new relationships, lifelong friends, happiness, introspection, and freedom from obsession. To me, my addiction is the greatest gift I have received. Who else can live a life of contemplation, introspection, self-love, discipline, and daily renewal? Recovery is living squarely in my frontal lobe.

TINSA Model Benefits

TINSA offers the clinician, the addict, and the partner hope, understanding, and a method to deal with all aspects of sobriety and recovery.

Benefits for the Clinician

- Provides understanding of the client's autonomic nervous system (ANS) and brain functioning.
- Provides understanding of the client's adverse developmental experiences (ADEs).
- Allows the clinician to see and understand how the client's ADEs have affected the brain and ANS.
- Allows the clinician to see the client's autonomic response to events and triggers.
- Demonstrates what the client has used as regulatory behaviors for self-regulation.
- Allows discernment between regulatory behaviors and addictive behaviors.
- Allows the clinician to teach the client healthy regulation.

Benefits for the Addict

- Gives the addict a clear understanding of how the brain and ANS work.
- Allows the client to see how he reacts to unprocessed events.

- Dramatically reduces shame through a deeper understanding of addiction as a brain disease.
- Teaches the client that he does have a choice in his addiction.
- Teaches the client healthy coping mechanisms to use when triggered.
- Teaches the client emotional regulation.
- Shows the client how ADEs are wounds that predisposed him to survival and addictive behaviors.
- Allows the client to uncover all of his triggers and provides a response to the hijacked brain.
- Provides a lifelong method of deeper recovery.

Benefits for the Partner

- Provides insight and relief to know why this is happening and that it is NOT her fault.
- Enables the partner to see addiction as a damaged system of coping rather than a character issue.
- Encourages the partner to use the TINSA model herself for emotional regulation.
- Provides a method for partner recovery.

Putting It Together

In the previous chapters, the reader learned about all the components of the TINSA model. In this chapter, we will show how TINSA is used in the treatment process. Using the TINSA model as a platform of treatment has enabled hundreds of clients to find sobriety and stay sober. In putting the pieces together, a brief overview will show what has been covered so that all the terms the TINSA model uses are clear and can be utilized by a client, a partner, or a therapist treating the addict.

The graphic below shows the placement of each component of the TINSA model and the feeling (sensation) states associated with each part of the foundation. This allows the client to become familiar with the terms used in the model. Included are the placement of ADEs, survival behaviors, and addiction. Using the foundation of regulation as the basis of this model allows clients to see exactly how their brains and bodies are reacting or responding. The graphic provides an overview of how their brains and autonomic nervous systems function and how they typically respond when threatened. It allows clients to explore, understand, and heal the adverse experiences that affected their brains and ANS, predisposing them to unconscious reactions rather than conscious response. By exploring the ADEs and the reactions to these events, the client can then understand how the trauma that occurred from his ADEs has created triggers (people, places, events, sights, sounds, memories, smells, or sounds) that ignite the sympathetic or dorsal reactions. We then focus on the regulatory behaviors the client has utilized throughout his lifespan as self-regulation and also show which of these regulatory behaviors have become addictive due to changes in the brain. Lastly, the model can be used to learn healthy coping and healthy self-regulation, thus enabling clients to live *within* their foundations. My clients learn to speak this language, practice, and when they speak of being in or out of their foundation, they know exactly what is happening to them in the present moment. They talk about a newfound ability to regulate in healthy ways and to deepen emotional competence.

TINSA uses the foundation of regulation to provide clients with a visual representation of how the brain and the autonomic nervous system react to stressful events. It demonstrates the three branches of the ANS, the ventral vagal response (calm/connected/safe), the sympathetic reaction (fight/flight/high freeze), and the dorsal vagal reaction (submit/narrowed consciousness/immobility/collapse). TINSA utilizes this approach to teach the client how his brain and body are reacting automatically and also how to gather control over these automatic reactions.

TINSA

TINSA Foundation of Regulation

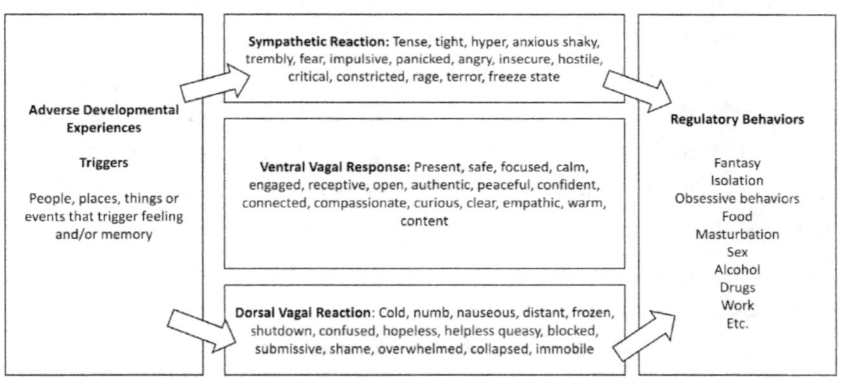

Adapted from Dr. Dan Siegel's model of *Window of Tolerance*. Originally found in *The Developing Mind* (2nd Ed). The Guilford Press, 2012. Used with permission. All rights reserved

Dorsal Vagal Reaction

The dorsal vagal is responsible for us going into a state of submission, shutting down into a restricted field of consciousness, becoming immobilized, or fully collapsing. The effects on the body include a sinking feeling in the gut, constriction of the pupils, possibly slumping over, and a very shallow and slow breathing rate. In some cases, there is the inability to move some parts of the body.

Patrick Weeg, a sensorimotor psychotherapist in Denver, Colorado, describes what happens during a dorsal vagal shutdown:

> People describe this as part of submitting, going along to get along. Making yourself smaller, literally curling into a ball to protect your vital organs from injury. Shame, self-loathing, hopelessness/helplessness, fragmentation of your sense of self. Feelings that your life is truly at threat of being extinguished—physically or psychologically. Physically, people feel numb, disconnected, spacey, "not here all the way," checked out, not aware. The muscles go limp, people feel unengaged and sometimes like a "robot," acting on auto pilot. At an extreme, fainting when the blood pressure decreases so much that it triggers a collapse and feigned death. You have an alteration of consciousness at times so it seems like you're looking down a tunnel with blinders on.
>
> Clients in this state either report being nauseous or actually vomiting. Also, the hearing can go—one man described it as "sounding like you're under water." This is tied in with the gut and the digestive system, so the bowels are often cleared at this point, muscles that hold in are released and people wet or defecate themselves here. (personal communication)

Ventral Vagal Response

We use the word *response* here purposefully. Unlike the other two brains, the ventral vagal is more aligned with the prefrontal cortex (frontal lobe) and our Broca's area, which is responsible for words. When the ventral vagal is engaged, we are integrated cognitively, emotionally, and bodily, which means we are able to integrate information from all three without becoming flooded. When we are in the foundation, our ventral vagal is doing a very good job of keeping us calm and present. This is where our authenticity and our vulnerability occur. We accurately identify threats, real or perceived. If there is a threat, we respond consciously rather than reacting unconsciously. Notes Weeg,

> Here people are able to think and feel their feelings but not be overwhelmed by and flooded with them. They can have very strong feelings, but still feel present. In this state, people are alert but relaxed, they are able to 'observe' their experience while having it. It is sometimes called the 'Integrated Zone.' Individuals are able to speak and then shift rapidly to listening by engaging the inner ear muscles and muscles of the throat. People describe this as feeling alert and related to their body at the same time. (personal communication; note the words associated with a ventral vagal in the foundation response)

Sympathetic Reaction

Sympathetic reaction uses brain chemicals to get the body ready for action. Epinephrine and norepinephrine speed up the heart rate, muscles tense up, and breathing becomes more rapid. Our palms get sweaty, and our mouths dry up. We are either ready to fight or have the overwhelming sense to run.

Adverse Developmental Experience

Adverse developmental experiences, or ADEs, are experiences that happen throughout the lifespan; however, their origins take place from before birth through the formative years and have both biological as well as emotional and psychological effects. An ADE is any person, place, thing, or event that causes a person's brain and nervous system to malfunction in human relationships, leaving the person with an isolated self-regulatory system of emotional regulation and need gratification. ADEs cause deep and lasting wounds. Primarily we see three types of wounds that occur with our clients: wounds while powerless, wounds where we were controlled or had forced regulation by an outside force, and wounds because there was little to no regulation present.

Wounds of powerlessness happen with emotional, physical, or sexual abuse where we were overpowered and had no means of escape. These wounds usually set up the system to use freeze as a primary coping mechanism later in life because it was the only way to survive at the time of the event. Powerlessness wounding can also set a person up to be sympathetically based by being hyperaware of threats that are associated with the original adverse experience. These wounds deeply impact our ability to be vulnerable and form healthy bonds with others.

Controlled or forced regulation damages a person's ability to be authentic. A child whose parents are emotionally controlling, strict, judgmental, or compare the child's worth to others or an outside system of worth (sports, money, grades, for example, or telling their children how they should live instead of exploring options and helping them solve their emotional distress) learns to shut down and suppress emotions. This type of wound usually constructs a sympathetic reaction system, where emotions are bottled up and then are expressed either through rage or in some type of acting out or addiction.

Finally, we see people wounded from not receiving enough regulation or any regulation at all as children. Here we see the abandonment and neglect spectrum. These individuals were not taught how to feel, understand, regulate, or express emotions. They live with emotional incompetence, stuffing and then acting out to relieve the emotions.

This wound causes the person to develop invulnerability out of fear of losing emotional control or from the shame caused by not knowing how to be close and emotional. It also damages the person's ability to be authentic because authenticity requires mastery over our emotional lives.

ADEs create the client's triggers because ADEs cause trauma, and this trauma is stored in the midbrain. ADEs set up our systems to be different from those who have not had or were not as affected by ADEs. Because trauma makes our foundation shrink, we live in a constant state of anxiety or anger, or we live in an overwhelmed, numb, submissive state. Minor events, real or imagined, can set off our defense systems. All wounds caused through ADEs have several things in common: they halt or harm emotional development; they shrink a person's foundation, predisposing him or her to a system based on fight, flight, or freeze; they cause the person to become self-reliant and self-regulating with means outside of the self; and they produce triggers that, until disarmed with trauma therapy, act to chronically elicit defensive systems.

Trauma

Trauma is a term used to describe the impact that an overwhelming event has on the brain and autonomic nervous system. Trauma is the result of adverse developmental experiences. The lasting effects of our ADEs do not simply go away; they are permanently stored so that they stay with and trigger our unconscious brains to react. Trauma damages our ability to bond with others in any authentic or vulnerable way. Trauma, by nature, is associated with pain and is therefore the precursor to our regulatory and addictive behavior as a means to escape the unconscious pain.

As stated before, TINSA postulates that trauma is at the root of addiction. Overwhelming events that go unprocessed are stored in the unconscious midbrain. Survival depends on not doing something too dangerous twice, so our brains record these events as sensation and memory. Once activated, our systems will go into sympathetic reaction, and if the threat is large enough and we can't fight or escape, the dorsal reaction is triggered, and we freeze.

Triggers

A trigger is an experience (person, place, thing, event, thought, or sensation) that causes a person to involuntarily recall a previous traumatic or overwhelming memory. Triggers are trapped emotions that could not be processed at the time of the event. Trauma causes parts of the frontal lobe to go offline, and when this happens, the sensation and information of the event remain unprocessed. These stored memories and sensations can activate our defense systems, hijacking the brain and causing us to react rather than respond. When triggered, the conditioned response to fight/flight or freeze occurs and then unconsciously moves into a regulatory behavior to escape pain. Working with triggers is a major component in the TINSA model. However, we do much more than identify the triggers; we use trauma therapies to help desensitize and process the stored emotions.

Regulation Behaviors

Regulatory behaviors began as an early, unconscious attempt to regulate anxiety, fear, anger, depression, shame, or powerlessness when there was no caregiver to help the child resolve the turmoil, chaos, or lack of emotion that occurred early in life. While not all regulatory behaviors become addictions, all addictions start as regulatory behaviors. It is important to note that the main objective of our regulation behavior is to stop pain. Being outside of our foundation is painful. We self-regulate by using either a behavior or a substance to bring us out of a sympathetic fight-or-flight state or the feelings associated with this state, or we use regulatory behaviors to bring us out of our frozen state and kill the pain associated with the feeling or sensations of this state. Refer to TINSA Foundation of Regulation on page 111 to learn which feelings and sensations are found in these states.

Regulation behaviors can include the use of fantasy, isolation, food, work, technology, pornography, masturbation, sex, anorexia, or exercise, or they can be more about the use of substances, such as drugs and alcohol. Regulatory behaviors are something we do in order to feel better. Regulatory behaviors can also include thinking disorders such as being obsessive or compulsive. Even suicidal ideation can be a regulatory behavior because the goal is to get the pain to stop. Regulatory behaviors that do not become addictive—lying, deceit, manipulation, codependency, entitlement, or the need for control—often act as protectors to our addictions.

Foundation Expansion—Recovery

Recovery from addiction is the lifelong process of expanding our foundation, our ability to cope and remain calm *in healthy ways*. The culminating goal of TINSA is the healthy restoration of a person's ability to be vulnerable and authentic at all times. The goal is restoring integrity for the individual. The word *integrity* has its roots in the term *integer*, meaning "one," and the dictionary defines integrity as being whole and undivided. Addicts have two lives, a public life and a private life; recovery is having only one life. TINSA's aim is to help the client to learn how to know, understand, regulate, and express all of his emotions and be able to ask for his needs to be met. It also teaches the client how to protect, calm, and soothe the self in healthy, meaningful ways instead of relying on behaviors or substances that are meant to numb.

TINSA recovery is about being alive, being self-accepting, and having self-compassion. We work to return a person's ability for full intimacy. To be intimate requires absolute authenticity, and becoming authentic is hard work for an addict. In most cases, the new client doesn't really know himself because he has put on so many different masks over the years that his authentic being has atrophied. He has been what others wanted him to be from an early age. He has seen little in the area of being valued for who he is; instead, he was valued for what he did.

The other component of intimacy is vulnerability, which means that the client has to possess the ability to understand and handle his emotions. Shamed and remorseful clients often find hope when the only thing wrong with them is their inability to be vulnerable and authentic.

Foundation expansion is recovery. Most treatment models leave out this component, opting for controlling the addictive behaviors. According to TINSA, the addiction started through self-regulation and therefore can be much better managed by increasing one's ability to remain regulated. Foundation expansion starts with determining the current functioning of the individual. We have to assess how the client's system becomes hijacked and what he does to deal with the hijacking. We then immediately begin to teach healthy self-regulation to help the client stay present enough to consciously regulate his sensations, feelings, and thoughts. We teach the client how to "stay within his foundation" even in extreme circumstances. Foundation expansion greatly reduces the need for the regulatory and addictive behaviors, because the trigger is being eliminated. Teaching a person to live within a calm body sounds easy, but it takes much practice to undo years of living outside one's foundation.

Mindfulness is a huge component in the TINSA model. It means doing something on or with purpose. We are present to our environment and the people in it, and most of all, our bodies respond to these factors. Next, we begin to work on emotional competency, for most addicts have tried their whole lives to avoid or control their emotions. We work diligently to have our clients learn how to be present in their bodies and begin to identify even the subtlest sensations and feelings, for without emotional competency, vulnerability and authenticity are lost. Starting small pays large dividends. Meditation, yoga, deep breathing, connection with trusted friends and others in recovery, and long, slow walks all help a person to slow down and begin to learn emotional regulation.

Sobriety versus Recovery

I constantly remind my clients that there is a huge difference between sobriety and recovery. Addictive behaviors start out as regulatory behaviors, meaning they are the behaviors and substances found mostly through experimentation or by accident, which killed or temporarily relieved the roller coaster of emotions present when we have no other means by which to regulate our emotions. We learn or should learn the ability to regulate within the first three years of life. If we had parents or guardians who also lacked the ability to regulate or were unable to be present and allow their nervous systems to join and regulate ours, our ability to regulate fails to develop. When this occurs, we are left to regulate ourselves, and a system of self-regulation is born.

Staying free from these behaviors and substances is how most treatment and recovery programs define sobriety: "I am no longer participating in regulatory behaviors, and therefore all is well"—*not.*

In most current treatment modalities, the emphasis is placed on staying free from the behaviors. These therapies use skills to help addicts refrain from engaging in the behaviors or using the substances that once were destroying their lives. These modalities focus on the behaviors, not the cause. But if one desires to attain long-term, meaningful recovery, much more is needed for successful sobriety and recovery. If our regulatory behaviors are the direct result of adverse developmental experience, then simply stopping the behaviors will create a huge void by not addressing the problems that made us need to reach for regulation in the first place. In short, TINSA defines sobriety as stopping the behaviors and recovery as healing the cause.

In my experience and my work with addictions over the past thirty-one years, I have found both personally and professionally that addictive behaviors have to be stopped completely before the client can heal the core of the addiction. Any addictive use whatsoever will cause a delay in healing and may undo what was previously healed. In 1949, Canadian psychologist Dr. Donald Hebb coined the phrase "Neurons that fire together wire together." It is exactly for this reason that we must stop all behaviors associated with our addiction before we can rewire our brains.

If we do find the wounds that continually disrupt our regulation system, we find that the need or automatic response to regulate our nervous systems greatly diminishes. If we do not find and solve these core issues, we either return (usually sooner than later) to our self-regulation or find and use other regulation behaviors (addictions) to replace our old ways of coping.

I was sober in AA for twenty-two years, felt good, and thought I was on top of the world. Great career, house, nice car, friends, but for most of these twenty-two years I had kept hidden the fact that I had changed my drinking to sexual behaviors. I never got to the core. I simply found another way to blot out the pain stored from my unresolved adverse experiences. I had traded one addiction for another. Patrick Carnes labeled this "addiction interaction disorder." Because of my own experience, I often joke that if you scratch a person in AA, you will see underneath a sex-, food-, gambling-, or workaholic. And just like my alcoholism, the sex addiction took on a life of its own, with all the hallmarks of addiction: progression, escalation, tolerance, dissociation, and ultimately severe consequences that cost me my career and for a short while damaged my reputation. Once arrested, literally and figuratively, I sought treatment for my compulsive sexual behaviors. It was in this treatment that I began to understand the importance of looking deeper. I saw the value in exploring the importance of my experience in my family of origin and my early environment. However, I was still lacking the knowledge of how and why these early experiences had affected my life, predisposed me to addictions, and made me seamlessly transfer from one addictive behavior to another.

In many twelve-step meetings, people report that simple sobriety is not enough. It is common knowledge that we must seek out and be rid of the fundamental causes and conditions of our addiction, but few really do. In simple terms, sobriety is staying free of the behaviors and substances, while recovery is the lifelong process of healing that occurs once we have completely stopped using our automatic regulation responses. To do this we must reengage our frontal lobes. In my thirty-one years of recovery, I have witnessed countless people saying that staying sober is enough (denying the need for deeper work). They either stop their primary addiction and then become involved in another, or become men and women who are constantly angry, judgmental, dishonest, and controlling. They have continued to be on self-regulation and have become what are known in AA as "dry drunks."

With TINSA we go deeper than simply using sobriety as a phrase to relate that we are not using or acting out. Instead, we use *sobriety* and *sanity* interchangeably. *Merriam-Webster*'s definition of sanity, "soundness of mind," means that we are fully functioning in the frontal lobes, able to regulate the wildness created through unconscious reactions, pause long enough to survey the possible consequences of our actions, and make rational, healthy choices that promote bonding and intimacy rather than continuing with our self-serving, defensive survival reactions (*Merriam-Webster Online*, s.v. "sanity," accessed 2017, http://www.merriam-webster.com/). In TINSA we find and heal the events that were too overwhelming to process, thus making our brains and nervous systems susceptible to sympathetic and dorsal defense reactions. Recovery is stopping the survival behaviors *and* learning how to expand the foundation (your ability to interact in a real way with others) by removing stored trauma with protocols designed to allow the unresolved to resolve. We then can live in ways with people and activities that promote calm, connection, and a sense of safety, allowing us the ability to be authentic and vulnerable and ready for deep, intimate connections.

TINSA Sobriety—Slip versus Relapse

There appears to be great misunderstanding in the process addiction world with the terms *slip* and *relapse*. In the world of TINSA, there are relapses, and then there are behaviors that one engages in to promote, enhance, or justify the relapse, such as objectification, lying, manipulation, grooming, deceit, hiding, defensiveness, isolation, and ritualized behaviors. In the beginning of treatment for sexual addiction, there are no middle-of-the-road methods of sobriety. You either stop using your survival behaviors to regulate your brain and nervous system, or you don't. You are either sober, or you are not. We cannot get to the core of our addiction when our addictive behaviors are still operating. Sex addiction, and I would argue most process addictions, seem harder to stop than the substance addictions because with process addictions, our drugs are produced within our bodies. We don't have to walk into a liquor store or a bar to satisfy our addiction, but we can't very well live without our brains. For this reason, any behaviors that can lead to a relapse must be watched with vigilance in early sobriety.

I realize here that I may create controversy, but many skilled clinicians have come to agree: it seems that when it comes to many programs that treat process addictions, the term *slip* has caught on as a way for addicts to continue destructive behaviors without taking accountability for the fall. *Slip* was actually first used in Alcoholics Anonymous as a polite way of saying, "I returned to using alcohol last night." A slip meant and still means a relapse. A relapse is defined as a return of a disease or illness (behavior/substance) after a period of improvement, whereas a slip is defined as an unintentional and trivial mistake or fault or mistake in judgment (*Merriam-Webster Online*, s.vv. "relapse," "slip," accessed June 17, 2017, http://www.merriam-webster.com/).

As a recovering addict, I can tell you that once I knew better, I never once "accidentally" returned to beer, vodka, porn, or prostitution. A return to a behavior that has become addictive is *not* a slip; it is a relapse, and sobriety has been lost. We hold a hard line here because our ten years of empirical evidence have seen too many addicts try to justify their relapse as a slip. Clients will act out, and they believe it was a slip because "it only happened once, and it says on the Internet that because I stopped after only one time, I am okay." I invite you to run that rationalization by your spouse or partner and see how she responds.

In TINSA, *slip* and *relapse* are synonyms. A slip or relapse occurs anytime one engages in sexual behaviors that

1. increase dopamine to levels that produce a high;
2. are used to regulate emotional pain or avoid or escape from dysregulated emotions; and
3. return to any sexual behavior that is secret and that could produce harmful effects for the self or others.

Early and long-term sobriety and recovery have no room for justification. Far too often I have witnessed clients who continue in their addiction because they had a slip and did not see it as a problem. I am a recovering alcoholic, and if I say I had a slip because it was only beer, I am fooling myself. I have fully lost my sobriety and need to start over. I can't have *any* alcohol. And with sex addiction, I cannot engage in any of the sexual behaviors that I used that were harmful to myself, my loved ones, my family, or the community at large and consider myself sober.

For most of us, this means we stop using behaviors that are compulsive or in some way harmful: pornography; prostitution; massage parlors with documented sex-trafficked women; sex that is secretive and causes extremely painful betrayal trauma; compulsive masturbation causing self-injury, shame, self-loathing, and low self-esteem; strip clubs that propagate sexual objectification; and countless other means of nonconsensual, nonintimate gratification.

In our treatment definition, there is no difference between slips and relapses. When it comes to sex addiction, a slip is a relapse, and to call it otherwise has led to many addicts justifying their acting out for years.

Sex addiction sobriety and sex addiction therapists are not and will never be sex negative or religious zealots. We wholeheartedly support healthy, loving sexuality rather than sex that harms the self or others. The majority of certified sex addiction therapists are themselves in recovery. We do this important work because we have struggled through hell, found a solution, and want to share this solution with others. Sober is sober, and you will work with your therapist to carefully review your sexual behaviors to differentiate between healthy and unhealthy.

Eight

The TINSA program is designed to move the client from his self-regulated way of life to a life capable of mutual regulation with another human being. To do so, we utilize three distinct categories to help the client move through a process that engenders self-discipline, openness, honesty, transparency, authenticity, vulnerability, and trust.

For the addict, a person used to being in full control, vulnerability is a tall order. But by slowly moving from self-destructive self-regulation to outer-based regulation, and finally on to allowing others in, one realizes the essence of recovery. People who have been traumatized by adverse experiences usually shut down and develop a closed system of relating to others. Basically, these experiences disable a person's ability to trust anyone.

Addicts rely only on themselves. Addicts, having undergone trauma, *do not allow people in.* They keep people at arm's length, never allowing others to fully know the real person inside. Trauma does that. Until resolved, it makes a person forever skeptical of other people's motives, mostly with good reason. When you have been severely injured for just being your authentic self, you are going to think (or react) twice before doing that again. The same is true for vulnerability. Being hurt while vulnerable (without defense) causes our systems to be wary of vulnerability in the future. Many of my clients have been and are surrounded by people trying to love them, but they won't allow it.

TINSA is about repairing the original wounds that took away our ability to be vulnerable and our ability to be authentic. Once these wounds are repaired, we have the capacity for intimacy. In a recent termination session with a client, he blurted out through sobs, "I am okay, and I can let others love me." The goal of TINSA is to move the client from a self-regulated state to vulnerability, authenticity, and ultimately intimacy. In order for this to happen, the addict must first become aware of and stop using his well-fortified system of self-reliance.

Once people recognize and move through the following three stages, they are able to heal their wounds, become authentic, become vulnerable, and finally allow intimacy into their lives.

Stage One. Self-Regulated—No Ability to Regulate Other Than Addiction

People coming into treatment or returning after a relapse are stuck in self-willed thinking and behaviors. Up to this point, they have been doing everything on their own, living a life of isolation. This is really a survival mentality where emotions are seen as a liability instead of a healthy way of relating. The beginner doesn't trust others and does everything he can to not be fully known. In stage one, partners, family members, and friends see the addict as selfish, narcissistic, and self-absorbed. The addict new to sobriety lives in a defensive posture. Self-regulated people are dishonest, manipulative, secretive, scared, and highly sensitive to sympathetic or dorsal reactions. In many cases these individuals are like chameleons, changing into whatever people need them to be. The addict's primary way of relating to others is through self-regulated safety. Addicts do not delegate well because they have no trust in others. They think, "If anything is going to be done, or if I will ever get my needs met, then I must do it alone." Other thoughts that permeate the addict's mind may include the following: I have to make my life happen; relying on others is weak; I will be let down; I can't trust others; and I can't let you know me because if I do, you will reject me. The active and newly sober addict is self-centered in the extreme, but not in a mean or egotistical way; he is perceived as self-centered because he was groomed to look out for himself. In many cases no one had his back, or when he reached out for connection, it was not returned. Why trust anyone or anything? Even when addicts temporarily try to move to connect with others, the unresolved pain from early neglect, abandonment, and abuse sends them quickly back into self-regulation at the very hint of rejection or betrayal.

The self-regulation also includes the use of the addictive behaviors. Stopping the addiction causes psychological, mental, and physical pain. I have many clients swear that they will remain sober time and time again, only to return to their self-regulation as a means of coping. More often than not, this occurs because the client has never found any other way to cope. The primary go-to has been sexual thoughts and behaviors, usually for years. For the addict to move forward, however, the behavior must stop completely. The addict must fully realize that this system of self-regulation is a dead-end road. I tell my clients that there are roughly seven billion people on the planet, and we are designed to connect, not live in isolation. The good news is that by the time people reach my doors, they have had the rude awakening from a life lived for the self. Usually, people come in after their secret sexual life has been discovered. They are panicked and full of guilt and shame, but contained in this pain is a true awakening and the real beginning of healing.

Stage Two. Outer Regulation Is about Learning to Trust Something Stronger Than Ourselves

After we stop the destructive self-regulatory and addictive behaviors, we must begin to heal our dysregulation by relying on stronger nervous systems to heal our own. Addicts don't know healthy regulation. We find that we missed this crucial developmental step in our own lives because our parents and caregivers did not provide the adequate emotional nurturance and support needed for our nervous systems to develop properly. Without that support, we had to rely solely on the self. For recovery from sex or any other addiction to be successful, the ability to trust others has to be restored. The people who fail in recovery are never able give up their self-reliance, usually out of fear, and so they never develop the ability to trust. But once an addict fully understands that his self-regulated life hasn't worked and he is ready to accept help, true healing can begin.

In stage two the addict begins to trust others who have found their way through to recovery. Some are tenuous and skeptical, but the door seems to have been propped open. In this stage, people have the ability to practice authenticity, taking direction, allowing support, being vulnerable, and learning to identify, understand, regulate, and practice healthy expression of emotion. They begin to learn that they can finally see the authentic self. They practice honesty and integrity and are finally willing to follow the advice of those who have been where they are and made it through. Without this crucial leap, many addicts will soon return to a self-regulated life. Some fall during this time because the vulnerability is too great, or they are too inexperienced to regulate their mood, but those who get back up and continue to be open can and do heal their damaged nervous systems and find a sense of agency they never knew existed.

One of the best forms of outer regulation is joining a therapeutic treatment group for sex addiction with a certified sex addiction therapist (CSAT). These specialists are trained to recognize the nuances of intimacy disorders, while other well-meaning but untrained therapists miss the mark. Twelve-step meetings are another way to learn outer regulation. In these meetings we find other sufferers, and we find no judgment, ridicule, or condemnation. Twelve-step followers are a vast community of safe people with whom to experience trust, vulnerability, and authenticity, and more often than not, develop lives filled with real friends.

Outer regulation is when we learn to trust others enough to help us. We move from doing everything ourselves (the very method that got us into trouble) to allowing ourselves to stop running the show. Outer regulation is key in our practice of being vulnerable. Here we develop the ability to trust, to express our authenticity within safe environments.

Stage Three. Interregulation—True Intimacy

Interregulated is a term coined in my development of TINSA. Interregulation is synonymous with secure attachment. Attunement happens with others. Our brains and nervous systems attune outside of our conscious awareness, and for that to occur, we have to be with someone capable of attunement. Interregulation can never occur in active addiction or relapse. It is a dance between our system and another's system. We are no longer alone in a world filled with people; we are now in a state of mutual regulation: coregulation. We are not a brick wall keeping others out, nor are we overly dependent, inappropriately using others to regulate our moods. Interregulation can only occur between systems that are practiced at healthy regulation. In other words, interregulation happens between two secure systems. Humans are designed to coregulate, so the ability to do so is already built in; it just needs to be turned on.

Interregulation can be seen as two ventral vagal systems interacting, each producing a sense of calm, security, and connection in the other. Interregulation is not perfect, and even healthy systems sometimes move outside the foundation into a more defensive state. But when this occurs, we now have the capacity to help our partner return to a sense of calm instead of changing who we are to make the anger go away. In a primary relationship, it is crucial to be able to help regulate the partner. But it is not a matter of "fixing;" it means bringing her back to her own realization that she can get back within her foundation and operate from her frontal lobe rather than be stuck in the quagmire of reactive defenses born in the unconscious brain. The ebb and flow in interregulation is blissful. It is true attunement. Now the addict is able to see the partner's nonverbal requests, and the partner is able to see and meet the addict's. Interregulation not only creates safety, it provides security, trust, intimacy, and bonding.

TINSA allows full participation in treatment and recovery. When focusing on finding the adverse developmental experiences, we are particularly interested in finding the people, events, and places that damaged our abilities to be vulnerable or caused us to fear being fully authentic. We begin at birth and review the lifespan to the current age. Nothing is left unexamined. We are seeking the very seeds that grew into our broken ability with intimacy. We encourage our clients to actively participate in their own archeological adventure. Here we often encounter defensive loyalty to family systems that were less than nurturing. "My parents did their best. They gave me everything. How dare you say bad things about them!" Again, we reassure clients that we are not here to judge their parents or families; we are only interested in how they were affected by their early relationships and environments.

TINSA's Formula of Treatment

I have found in both my personal recovery and my professional life that finding and treating the core of addiction is essential in long-term sobriety and recovery. I could not stay sober through behavioral techniques alone. TINSA is a model that allows the addict to become responsible for his behaviors and learn to regulate emotions, something that should have occurred between the ages of birth and three years old but, for whatever reason, did not. TINSA allows each client to be active in the repair of his own hardwiring. Thus, the client can finally function on his own, this time with healthy behaviors.

Now that I have explained the model used at my treatment centers to heal sexual addiction, I will outline a greatly simplified version of the formula we follow, which has been met with great success and client approval using the tools and techniques found in the three stages listed below.

Stage one: Most new clients come in fully in self-regulation mode. To begin tackling their self-regulatory behavior, we employ the following steps to ready the client for further recovery. First, as with any addiction, we get the client off and away from the destructive sexual behaviors. We find and end each behavior that has been causing the client trouble. We educate clients on what to expect from their mind and body once they stop bombarding their brains with vast amounts of dopamine. We make them aware that for a while, it will be normal to experience anxiety, irritability, paranoia, agitation, and anger. We attempt to normalize their experience, helping them see that they have been ill and are now getting better.

Stage one consists of thoroughly educating the client as to how his brain and nervous system operate, providing clarity to the dysregulation he feels or has recently experienced. Doing so helps people see how their hardwiring, and not their character or personality, has been at play. A great deal of shame is reduced when they understand the hijacked system, and it gives them hope for a better way of life.

In this stage we also show the client how his brain and nervous system developed this manner of operation, how he became hardwired to defend instead of bond. The client learns that he has a damaged system but is not a damaged human being. We help him to find, build, and utilize people, places, and behaviors that allow his weary nervous system respite. We sow the seeds for emotional regulation to grow. Once a semblance of the skill of emotional regulation is in place, we can begin to turn our attention to what happened; what were the experiences, people, and other adverse experiences that clogged our ability to functional normally? Why are we unable to bond, express emotion, remain vulnerable, and have the deep knowledge of our worth that allows for full transparency, trust, and intimacy? We find and explore how our

ADEs have damaged our system and formed our perceptions, self-concepts, and deeply ingrained beliefs.

This is a process and does not happen overnight, although our most influential experiences are quick to emerge and begin a basis for understanding. To stay sober and recover fully, we need to survey the developmental experiences that caused us to rely on self-regulation and that adversely affected our ability to form bonds and trust intimacy. This is not about creating a list of what Mom and Dad (or anyone else) did wrong. It is an in-depth inventory of what happened to us and, more importantly, how these events affected us. Until we find these events and treat them in a later stage with trauma and somatic work, we are at risk of repeating the cycle.

We are not simply looking for experiences where only bad happened, but as Gabor Maté (2010) states, we look for where not enough good transpired. Moving from self-regulation to interregulation requires that we find and heal the trauma that was stored from our unresolved ADEs. Until this trauma is processed and healed, it will always be available to take us out of our foundation in dissociation and leave us vulnerable to acting out.

As stated earlier, TINSA is a bottom-up approach, meaning that we work directly with how the brain works and how information first enters our brain. A bottom-up approach works directly with the limbic and reptilian complexes, the seat of trauma and addiction. The other approach, a top-down approach, deals with our thinking brain. Many clients have spent years talking with therapists about their issues, tried solution-focused techniques, cognitive behavioral approaches, behavioral modifications, or other methods that work directly with the frontal lobe. These techniques, while helpful in combination with TINSA, by themselves are usually ineffective.

TINSA uses the newest scientific research to find and treat addiction, as well as its manifestation and causation. Trauma protocols include eye movement desensitization and reprocessing (EMDR); brainspotting, which is another form of desensitization and reprocessing; somatic experiencing (SE), which helps unresolved and stored trauma relapse and process through the body; sensorimotor psychotherapy, similar to SE, which finds and enables the client to release and process trauma from the body; and finally, dialectical behavioral therapy, which utilizes skills the client has to gain a conscious choice over subcortical reactions. Stage one culminates with much understanding and a great deal of healing, enabling the client to regulate the self in much healthier ways. Now that healing has begun to occur, the client must begin practicing these newfound systems of regulation with others in a safe and nonjudgmental atmosphere; here we move into stage two.

Stage two: After a client has learned about his regulatory system and how it was affected, and has begun healing the larger triggers that cause autonomic hijacking, he has a sense of regulation and hope. But if healthy self-regulation were the only goal, he would still be managing himself, just in a different way. Stage two is about giving up self-reliance. Here our clients actively begin to work with others who also were once closed off and isolated.

In my practice I have multiple groups focused only on learning how to practice authenticity and vulnerability. The practice of vulnerability is, by definition, our ability to live without defense. In my groups, people learn to accept that they still try to live defensively. Allowing others to call us out on our intimacy-blocking beliefs and behaviors allows us to soften and be more aware of our automatic responses. We show up as we are, and if we are playing out an old, unconscious role formed in the past, we let others bring it to our awareness. Being with others who are recovering from the same condition allows us to feel heard and accepted instead of judged. We learn that we can accept help and be appreciative that others have our best interests in mind.

Here we also show up as our authentic self, allowing others, sometimes for the first time, to see exactly who we are. We practice honesty and transparency and have no secret self out front, protecting us from feared rejection. Stage two allows us to find self-acceptance and really come to believe that we are not bad or flawed individuals, but rather former addicts who were trying to avoid pain. For the first time since our wounds caused us to close down, we let others in, learning that we do deserve love and that we can ask for what we need. We have now formed a support network with other recovering addicts to find a place of acceptance, nonjudgment, and intimacy. We can practice our regulation skills with others, become emotionally competent, and begin to form true bonds with others. We have experienced true intimacy.

Stage three: This is the final transition from self-regulation to consistent intimacy with others, including our families, our wives and partners, and the rest of humanity. We no longer have to live in a world of isolation. We have learned how to feel and regulate our emotions, we have learned to seek help, and we have learned to let others in without a constant fear of rejection. Most importantly, we are our authentic selves, the people we were before our ADEs and their effects on our systems and self-beliefs. Stage three is a lifelong endeavor. There is no destination other than the continued practice of emotional regulation and full human expression.

If this sounds too easy, relax; it is actually extremely difficult, especially when the reconnection with our loved ones may be met at first with disdain, disbelief, skepticism, and at times, rage. We did what we did, no denying that, but we can atone for our past by staying regulated and owning and repairing what we have destroyed. We no longer make excuses for our behavior; instead, we take accountability for all we have done and all we will do. This is freedom. This is recovery.

To utilize the foundation model, we list the substances and behaviors that we have used and that we must remain free of in order to heal the wounds that caused us to need these substances and behaviors in the first place. We list the things we use or used in an attempt to reduce sympathetic charge, increase parasympathetic charge, or resolve the trauma stored through sexual, physical, or emotional abuse. These behaviors, of course, include our sexual behavior, but they can also be gambling, food, electronics, video games, work, obsession, alcohol, drugs, or a plethora of other possibilities. These are the behaviors we MUST stop. We cannot get to the treatment modalities used here when the system is still being regulated through behavioral or substance avoidance.

Nine

For the Partner

Lies, Secrets, and Betrayal

In a recent therapy session, the partner of a sex addict stated that the current literature concerning sex addiction and betrayal trauma contains great explanations of what happens with betrayal trauma but doesn't tell you what to do about it. Hopefully, this chapter will help you begin to take back your power and find safety, and will leave you with the ability to make well-rounded, conscious decisions.

For the betrayed partner, the newly discovered sexual infidelity causes immense pain. However, the real devastation comes from the secret life: the lies, the hiding, the manipulation, the duplicity, and the total destruction of the partner's perceptions and reality. Intimate betrayal is the definition of an adverse developmental experience. The addict's behaviors have caused damage that will forever influence how the betrayed partner's brain and nervous system will respond to trust and intimacy.

Time after time, as a new couple comes into my office, I have witnessed the betrayed partner sit in numbness and pain trying to wrap her head around the discovery of the secret life. You, the partner, feel as if a bomb has just gone off. Your world has just exploded, and there is no safety to be found. You are experiencing the trauma of betrayal.

Perhaps you were emptying his pockets to do the laundry and found a business card for a sensual massage. Or you logged in to the computer to retrieve a recipe and got a porn site that he forgot to dump. Or you were paying your bills online, when a chat room popped up and Angel 321 asked if it was safe to talk.

There is no way to process the overwhelming new information you just found, usually by accident, hoping against hope that it is not true. You confronted him, and he lied. You showed him your proof, and he lied. If you are lucky, he finally will admit he has been unfaithful, but somehow you know you are only seeing the tip of the iceberg. I see, time and time again, sex addicts come in with their partner, claiming they want to change, they finally see the light, only to start resisting by saying things like "it's too much money," "let's think about it," or "this is going to cost me too much time away from work." I see the hope slowly dim in the eyes of the partner, who wants to believe that the addict really wants to change and things will be different.

I hate to be blunt, but unless the addict is willing to do anything suggested to him by the certified sex addiction therapist—if he resists or defends in the smallest way—there is much more to the story of his addiction than he is willing to share. I was recently working with a couple where the man told his wife he was only into pornography. After I discussed with them an intensive program that would best build a foundation for healing the man, he resisted and resisted, although his wife really wanted it. It came out subtly that the addict was terrified to discuss his sexual behaviors in front of his wife. In cases like these, there is always more that you, the partner, do not know, and it is your total right to know everything.

I also cannot emphasize enough that what you are feeling and experiencing is normal. Your brain and nervous systems are doing exactly what they are designed to do: protect you. In the past when you felt something was wrong and you questioned him, he denied it, deflected, blamed you, or told you that you were crazy. We call this "gaslighting," the complete denial or invalidation of your perceptions and your reality. You are not crazy; your nervous system is doing exactly what it is supposed to do in the presence of a life-threatening event (yes, this *is* a life-threatening event), and the way your brain is reacting is probably terrifying to you. You may feel like killing him; you may punch him or throw things; you may scream and yell profanities and threaten to destroy him—all normal reactions to the trauma the intimate betrayal has caused. Please don't act on your feelings, but know that feeling them doesn't make you bad or crazy. This reaction makes you normal.

"Great," you say. "Knowing I am normal doesn't help with the pain, the devastation, or the utter feeling of hopelessness." Many partners state that their world and everything they know has completely shattered. They don't know what to believe, whom to trust, or where to turn. This is called betrayal trauma—a type of trauma that means the person you bonded with the most, whom you trusted the most, has just betrayed you in the most devastating way possible. It doesn't matter if the betrayal occurs through discovering your partner is using pornography, chat rooms, massage parlors, having an affair, or seeing prostitutes; the devastation is the same. And although it certainly is not insignificant, most partners report that the sex is the least of the problems: the real devastation comes from the deceit, the lies, and the secret life.

What you are now experiencing is the very definition of an adverse developmental experience, an event that is so overwhelming that there is no way to process it. Your brain and nervous system have now been permanently altered. Right now, you might be numb, in shock, and terrified, or you might come out of the frozen state to feel your rage, or every fiber of your being is screaming, *run*! These reactions are happening because your frontal lobe is disengaged. Your solution will be to use the following recommendations to restart your frontal lobe.

Know Your Reactions

Know that you have experienced an event that has caused a threat to your life. Your response is normal, you are not crazy, and yes, these feelings will end. Right now, as Dr. Barbara Steffens, coauthor of the book *Your Sexually Addicted Spouse: How Partners Can Cope and Heal* (Steffens and Means 2009), points out, partners are seeking to be safe in a place where there is no safety. I want to help you to get back to a sense of security as soon as possible, and the first place you can find this security is within yourself.

As you have read by now, this book contains a proven method for helping people to be aware of, understand, regulate, and express their emotions in healthy ways by understanding how their automatic systems are reacting to this life-threatening event. By using the foundation, you can look to see how this threat has impacted you and is continuing to cause you issues, how past betrayals and ADEs have now come alive again, and how to manage yourself in healthy ways that can help you make clear decisions on how to proceed with your relationship and your life.

Adverse Effects to Your Systems

A life threat will cause your autonomic nervous system to do one of two things. Either you will rage, fight, yell, scream, kick, scratch, bite, threaten, tell everyone you know, and maybe even kick him out of the house, or, if the threat is large enough, your autonomic system will shut down, causing you to freeze and to feel overwhelmed, numb, confused, disoriented, and unable to respond. This response brings feelings of helplessness, hopelessness, disassociation, and utter powerlessness. Your ANS is doing this to keep you alive and protect you from what has just caused massive injury to your well-being. It is important here to notice where you are: Are you angry or wanting to run, are you shut down and immobile, or are you experiencing a combination of the two? It is very helpful to see that your brain and your body are reacting in a very normal way to a subversive experience. Breathe: you are having a reaction to a life-threatening event; you are *not* the sum of your feelings. Where are you now? Use the diagram below daily, minute by minute, if you need to see how your brain and nervous system are reacting to this discovery. If you notice the sensations in your body, notice your feelings, notice your thoughts, and *allow* them to be—they will change. In mindfulness terms, be curious to see how these sensations ebb and flow, how they change, and what they make you want to do. Our goal here is to get you out of your limbic brain—your reactive brain—and into your frontal lobe—your thinking, aware, planning, and real safety brain.

Partner Foundation

Sympathetic: Tense, tight, hyper, anxious, fearful, burning, shaky, trembly, obsessive, impulsive, panicked, insecure, hostile, critical,

Frontal Lobe: Warm, open, calm, connected, engaged, present, happy, hopeful, expansive, tender, confident, happy, powerful, safe, trusting, optimistic, positive, creative, playful, valuable

Parasympathetic: Cold, numb, dizzy, frozen, hollow, disconnected, spacey, heavy, queasy, nauseous, stuck, hopeless, helpless, blocked, confused, submissive

In a clinical study, Barbara Steffens and R. Rennie (2006) found that up to 70 percent of partners of sex addicts met all the criteria for a diagnosis of post-traumatic stress disorder. Common symptoms of PTSD include the following:

- intrusive thoughts
- nightmares
- flashbacks
- being reminded of discovery
- numbing or absence of emotional response
- reoccurring reminders or images
- inability to recall key parts of the discovery
- overly negative thoughts and assumptions about oneself or the world
- exaggerated blame of self or others for causing the trauma
- negative affect
- decreased interest in activities
- feeling isolated
- irritability or aggression
- risky or destructive behavior
- hypervigilance
- heightened startle reaction
- difficulty concentrating
- difficulty sleeping

PTSD can be diagnosed if you are experiencing the abovementioned symptoms, and they have been consistent for a period of four weeks.

Past Trauma

Some partners experience a double hit to an already fragile nervous system. Partners who previously experienced the trauma associated with earlier ADEs are predisposed to a more adverse reaction to the betrayal trauma. Earlier betrayals; abandonment; neglect; sexual, emotional, or physical abuses; or being raised in an alcoholic or other addicted family can make your recovery more challenging. When a new trauma occurs, all old, unresolved trauma is lit back on fire. Robert Scaer (2014) calls this kindling, like the very flammable material used to start a bonfire. Your brain's number-one job is to keep you alive, and it will now tell you that a past threat has reemerged and is in your living room! Some psychologists call this complex posttraumatic stress disorder (CPTSD). It has become complex because the earlier traumas were never resolved or processed out of the midbrain. CPTSD has many of the same qualities as PTSD, but with the difference that traumatic events repeat throughout the life span. In this case, many sufferers feel they are trapped in a never-ending, negative cycle. The following characteristics are associated with CPTSD:

- chronic or repeated traumas of the same nature
- flashbacks
- a fragmented sense of self
- a desire to isolate
- severe affect dysregulation
- insomnia
- desire to avoid the relationship
- being hyperalert
- preoccupation with the addict's every move
- being chronically overwhelmed
- inability to contain emotional outbursts

Regardless of which type of PTSD you are experiencing, your number-one priority is safety. Since partners are looking for safety where none exists, the best possible source of safety is what is within *your* control—you.

Safety First

The most important question is this: What do I need right now to feel safe right now? Asking yourself this question over and over will help you stay within your foundation and do your reasoning with the thinking part of your brain (your frontal lobe). It will also provide relief from the midbrain, where everything is an emergency. There are some very good tools to help keep you squarely in your frontal lobe, or "within your foundation." Recovery for you means that you will expand your ability to stay present, regulated, calm, and able to employ your thinking brain more each day. As with most partners, you will become angry and resentful that your life has come to "regulating your own nervous system," but practicing this regulation will pay large dividends very soon. Many well-meaning but untrained therapists will try to talk you through your emotional upset, but as mentioned previously, talk therapy will do little to relieve the constant onslaught of sensations, feelings, and thoughts your midbrain is happy to provide. Safety comes from first calming down your reptilian and limbic systems, and this is done with specialized therapies, not talk.

Triggers

A trigger is defined as a sight, smell, sound, thought, person, or felt sense that alerts your nervous system that you are in danger. It is when we recall a previous painful experience, and our automatic protection systems take over. Triggers form when something very painful was experienced and *was not resolved*. It is our own natural protection system doing its job. If you are hiking in the woods and almost step on a rattlesnake, your brain is going to remember this experience because it was very threatening. The next time you go on your walk, you are going to be hyperaware of anything that might resemble a snake. It is the same with betrayal trauma. When betrayed through sexual infidelities, your brain will remember and set up an automatic response to anything that was associated with your discovery. You may now be triggered by his phone, computer, workplace, or places where he has acted out. Suddenly everything is suspect as you recall other times that you have been in danger. You will be triggered when he is not home or is home alone, when he goes to work or shuts down and seems distant.

Triggers are healthy in that they keep you from further danger; however, life becomes a nightmare when you are triggered by everything in your life and you cannot determine if the trigger is real or just a false alarm.

Finding Your Reaction

In my experience, most of my clients have a go-to method of survival. Quite often these were set in very early years. Those who have experienced severe ADEs during the first three years of life will be subject to an automatic freeze response when confronted with a threat. People who freeze during a threat appear confused, shut down, distant, disassociated, numb, or depressed. In essence they become immobile, unable to respond to what is happening.

After discovery, most partners will be in this state for quite some time. Unsure of how to respond, their brains will fall back on their earliest form of defenses, perhaps staying stuck in a hyperactive sympathetic state, constantly waiting for the other shoe to drop, being hypervigilant of their surroundings, being unable to stop obsessively thinking and asking questions about the sexual betrayal, and experiencing feelings of bitter sadness, disbelief, terror, and rage. Adversely, they may stay completely numb, disoriented, shut down, confused, and forgetful, and may feel that they are unable to go on. Everyday tasks at home become seemingly impossible for them, let alone being able to work, tend to the children, and even socialize.

Betrayal touches every part of your world, and it seems it will never end. You may experience deep feelings of shame and embarrassment, anger at yourself for even considering staying, and loneliness, wondering, "Who can I talk to about this?" You may take your partner's betrayal as a measure of your physical, mental, or emotional worth. You are wounded to the core. The good news (if you're willing to call it that) is that you are not alone. There are thousands of women facing the same challenge, and you can find them for support. You will come to learn that this never was or is about your worth, your looks, your weight, or your intelligence. This is ONLY about your partner's total inability to be authentic and vulnerable. It is absolutely not your fault in any form. Your goal for healing is to heal yourself. It is to understand how this betrayal has dramatically affected the way your brain and your nervous system are going to respond for quite some time. In the next chapter, I will outline a formula that will absolutely let you know if your partner is doing the work to become trustworthy and deserving again of your trust and love. By now most partners have heard all the words and all the promises. But to stay safe, you can only look at actions and again finally return to trusting your intuition. You will know if your addict partner is changing.

Making It through the Crisis

Using the diagram above, check often to see how your nervous system is responding to the threats or triggers that occur. Look for the words associated with each system that match your body's sensations or feelings to determine if you have been hijacked by your sympathetic system (fight/flight) or your parasympathetic system (freeze/numb).

Once you locate your reaction, you can use the techniques below to help yourself regulate your nervous system.

Emergency Techniques to Restore Calm

At first it will feel as if you are on the highest, deepest, most terrifying rollercoaster on the planet. One moment you will be up; the next moment you will be plunged into despair. The following techniques will help you survive the large waves that seem to keep knocking you down. Using these techniques, either in isolation or in combination, will help return you to a state of calm and balance. In the beginning you may have to employ these techniques many times per day, but they will work if you use them. Remember, what has just happened has stolen all your power; now it is time to begin restoring your power.

These techniques were found by using the research of others in helping the autonomic nervous system become more regulated. Many are from the amazing founder of dialectical behavioral therapy (DBT), Dr. Marsha Linehan. Remember if you can to notice how you feel before each technique and how you feel after the technique—you are restoring your own safety.

The TIP Technique

TIP is an acronym for temperature, intense cardio, and progressive relaxation. It goes without saying that you will employ these techniques only if they do not exacerbate a preexisting condition such as a heart problem or physical limitation.

Temperature

We like to employ the use of ice, either as ice cubes, ice packs, or instant cold packs, to guarantee a speedy return to easier regulation. Patients find it virtually impossible to be out of their foundation while holding an ice cube. The same effect can occur from running your hands under cold water or splashing cold water on your face. This technique invigorates the ventral vagal nerve that is responsible for your feelings of calm and safety. Use every time you feel yourself losing control, needing to know answers right now, or when you are filled with rage or simply too frightened to move. Ice activates what is known as the dive reflex, what the body would do if it were actually freezing and begins to shut off unneeded areas of the brain. Panic is not needed for survival, so this will be calmed down.

Intense Exercise

Intense exercise means you are going to fully bring on your sympathetic system, and thus automatically activate your parasympathetic system (the calm portion). Intense cardio can be a set of jumping jacks, running up and down stairs, dancing, or doing short sprints.

Progressive Relaxation

There are several suggestions for this technique, but I have found that the one mentioned here works better than others. If we are to employ trying to feel calm by relaxing one body part at a time, those stuck in the freeze state will not benefit as much as those in fight and flight. Instead, I suggest that patients tense and relax one body part at a time, focusing on the feeling when letting go or relaxing.

5-4-3-2-1 Technique

Our next suggestion for emotional safety employs mindfulness. You will bring yourself back in your foundation (your frontal lobe and body) by using your five senses. This technique can be done anywhere and at any time.

Name out loud or to yourself

- five things (or colors) you see around you;
- four things you can feel outside of your body (e.g., room temperature, feet on floor, bottom in the chair);
- three things you can hear;
- two things you can smell; and
- one thing you can taste.

We often employ the use of essential oils for the smelling portion, and gum or mints for the tasting portion. These items are easily transportable and will enhance the experience.

Deep Breathing

When we are out of our foundation, we will either hyperventilate or breathe very shallowly or hold our breath. Restricting our air will keep the unconscious part of our brain activated as a way to survive. The frontal lobe—our thinking brain—takes a tremendous amount of fuel, including oxygen, so deep, slow breaths will help us return to a sense of calm.

When Not in Crisis

Soon there will be times when you find yourself relatively stable for days at a time. At this point, you can begin to expand your foundation. Doing so will enable you to better weather the times when you are triggered and you feel knocked off your feet. Using your own foundation, how you normally respond to crisis will provide you answers on which techniques to help you expand your tolerance and regulation in healthy ways. Use the following techniques to continue to expand your ability to regulate your foundation (your emotions) based on how you normally react to crisis.

For both the partner and the addict, TINSA's definition of recovery is doing activities and being with people that expand your foundation in healthy ways.

Continued Foundation Expansion

Being in your foundation is synonymous with being in your frontal lobe. As described earlier, if we are to be in our foundation, our triune brain must be acting in harmony. The unconscious and conscious portions are operating in unison without unconscious hijacking. As we learn to become aware and manage our own systems of hyper- and hypo-arousal, we can focus more on the people and activities that help us expand our ability to tolerate triggers and setbacks. The following are suggestions to use for expanding your foundation, enabling you to feel more powerful, in control, and stable, all while helping your thinking brain make good decisions based on reality and not fear or anger.

Establish Support Network

It is sad but true that many partners find it very difficult to find people who can support them through this time. Many well-meaning friends and family members offer too much advice and not enough real support. The last thing you need is a judgmental friend or family member telling you to run when your heart has not yet decided. It is imperative to find supportive, nonjudgmental people who can listen and empathize without lecturing you or telling you what to do.

With the advent of the Association of Partners of Sex Addicts Trauma Specialists (APSATS), this type of support is springing up all over the nation, either in person or through phone or Internet support groups and meetings. Here you will be guided by a trained partner specialist who helps members deal with the trauma of betrayal. There are also support networks that are offshoots of the twelve-step support networks of Sex Addicts Anonymous (SAA) called Codependents of Sex Addicts (COSA) as well as the partner support groups of Sexaholics Anonymous (S-Anon). A word of caution here, however: many of our partners have reported not faring well with COSA. Anything that assumes that the partner is part of the problem by labeling her as "codependent" will not provide the needed relief and regulation required for recovery. Your best bet for support with others who are also experiencing this betrayal trauma is to find an APSATS-trained therapist and ask for a support group. As far as friends and families go, we suggest that you ask yourself the following questions: Is the person I am about to tell worthy of my trust? Are they part of my inner circle? Will they keep my confidence or spread this news all over the neighborhood or throughout my family?

In the next chapter, I will provide the addict suggestions of what is absolutely needed to get sober, stay sober, and begin full recovery. I will also outline for the partner what the addict must be doing—not saying—to reestablish safety and trust so she can know without a doubt that it is safe to resume trust and decide if she wishes to stay in the relationship.

Ten

SURVIVING DISCOVERY

Michael Barta Ph.D., LPC, CSAT-S

S ex addiction is a condition that needs to be treated by therapists who have extensive training in this specific area. The good news is that the occurrence of high-profile cases within the media and the ensuing visibility of this disease have made more people begin to seek help for compulsive and addictive issues related to sex. The bad news is that ANYONE can say they treat sex addiction even though they may have no special training or experience with this unique issue.

If you are reading this book, most likely you are either seeking help with sex addiction or are currently seeing a therapist for this issue. It cannot be emphasized enough that if you are facing sex addiction, you should explore your options with specialists who treat sex addiction. To find the right therapist, look for what is known as a certified sex addiction therapist, or CSAT. These therapists have completed rigorous training through the International Institute for Trauma and Addiction Professionals (IITAP). Partners of sex addicts should look for an APSATS, trained by the Association of Partners of Sex Addicts Trauma Specialists. Both the CSAT and the APSATS treat all stages of the addiction. For too long I have heard horror stories of people working with therapists who state they "treat" sex addiction. Partners have been told to "just have more sex" with the addict to "fix" the addiction, and addicts have been told that "your partner is part of the problem." I have also seen therapists, sex addicts themselves, untrained and not in recovery, try to work with sex addicts, with disastrous results.

This is about caution; this is about finding a specialist. You would not go to a general practitioner to treat your stage-four cancer, so why go to a generalist to treat your extraordinary addiction and relationship problems?

In the next few pages, I will provide a blueprint for surviving what is most likely the most painful, devastating, heartbreaking time of your life. I have developed and used this template over the past decade to minimize the impact of the betrayal, reduce the shame of the addict's exposure, and help the addict take the lead in helping his betrayed wife or partner heal, regain trust, and experience the true intimacy she has always wanted.

Partners heal through seeing actual change in the addict—not with what he is saying or doing, but by how he is being and how he is changing. A lot of my patients are frustrated when they complain they are doing everything right, but the partner is still not satisfied. That is because sobriety is *doing*; recovery is *being*. Your end goal here is a lifelong pursuit of authenticity and vulnerability. Sobriety is but the starting point. Actual change comes through learning to be your true self and sharing that true self with your partner.

Often the advent of discovery brings about feelings of hopelessness, fear, rage, and disbelief. At such times one cannot expect the partner to be able to rationally calm her own emotions or stay within her frontal lobe. It is important, however, that as soon as possible, safety is established for the partner and for the addict. Although the pain is overwhelming, and it is understandable that the partner feels trapped, humiliated, shamed, and terrified, physical violence can never be justified. To survive discovery, the couple has to adhere to two nonnegotiable principles.

The first nonnegotiable principle is that physical assault or violence cannot be an option. This includes hitting, slapping, punching, kicking, throwing items, hair pulling, or other behaviors intended to cause physical harm. Many partners have admitted with embarrassment and shame that when they found out about the sexual betrayal, they were so full of rage that this was their first response. While some see this as justified, it is not. No matter what has occurred, no one deserves physical violence. This is not just to protect the addict; it protects the partner as well. It only takes one person to report physical violence, and now a domestic violence charge is added to the mess.

The second nonnegotiable principle that we highly encourage is to stay away from emotional abuse. This includes yelling and swearing, name calling and insults, threats and intimidation, ignoring and excluding, publicly shaming or embarrassing, or any other behavior that is intended to cause emotional pain. What you are feeling is normal, and it is important to remember that you have a choice now in how to respond to these painful feelings.

Recovery Timelines

It is important to know that it takes a great deal longer for the partner to recover than it does the addict. It is imperative that the partner be given as much time and space as needed to fully recover if there is any hope for trust to be rebuilt. The addict has lived with his addiction for as long as he can remember, but it is new information for the partner. When discovered, the addict feels shame, guilt, remorse, and fear, but it is not uncommon for him to also feel a tremendous amount of relief because he no longer has to hide his secret life. He has hit bottom. If he engages in a rigorous program of recovery, he will get better quickly. Fortunately, there are a lot of options for treatment for the addict. Sex addiction treatment has been evolving for the past thirty years. The addict can see a certified sex addiction therapist, find a sex addiction group, join numerous twelve-step meetings for sexually compulsive behavior, and find overwhelming support.

Things are different for the partner. She has just discovered that the person she has been with has a secret life and is not who she thought he was. It is not uncommon for the wife to feel like she has never known the person she believed she knew and trusted. Recovery options for partners are improving but still severely lag behind the help that is available for addicts. It is not uncommon for recovering addicts to feel good and happy about their newfound recovery, while partners feel left out and unfairly treated.

I often hear a partner state, "Yep, it's all about him again." There is a reason for this discord. For the addict, the most important thing to remember is that it is going to take a very long time for your wife or partner to heal from the betrayal and pain you have caused. Discovery may provide relief for the addict because the burden of his secrets has been lifted, but at the same time, the partner is feeling horror at a world being turned upside down.

I see all too often that after a few months, the addict feels that the partner should be doing better, that she should hurry up and get over this. That she should be further along in her therapy for her recovery. This is a recipe for divorce, because at this point, the addict just wants everything to return to normal, and the partner no longer knows the meaning of that word. What is important in surviving this time is patience. The addict has to take the responsibility in order for his wife or partner to recover. Outlined here is the ability to make this time more productive and lead to the rebuilding of trust.

Am I an Idiot for Staying?

A majority of the partners I treat wonder if they are fools for wanting to stay and see if things can work out. They also report feeling as if their whole life and relationship with the partner has been a complete lie. And speaking for the addict here, I can assure you that although there were times that he was present and emotionally bonded with you, his problem was that he could not maintain that emotional bond because of previous negative experiences with bonding. But, in the over fifteen hundred people I've treated since my inception as a CSAT, I have witnessed only six divorces with couples that have come in for treatment. I do not think this is rare or because of any special skill I have, but instead it speaks to the willingness to see this as a real disease that can be treated. Within these couples' lives, things have not been easy, and the number-one cause of continued discord is the addict not following his treatment plan. There have been occasions, too, where a partner has been so wounded by the betrayal that she has refused to do her own healing. This has also caused understandable distress, but by far, the addict's healing, transparency, honesty, and ability to remain nondefensive is the greatest source of safety and the reestablishment of trust.

Weren't You Thinking of Me?

This question has been asked hundreds of times with the couples I see. When asked, the addict usually stares blankly into space with no idea how to answer. The truth is that while in active addiction, the addict was not thinking of you, the kids, his career or reputation, possible consequences, being discovered, being arrested, or how his own worth would suffer from another bout of acting out. Addiction is formulated and carried out in the unconscious brain as an attempt to avoid a dysregulated nervous system. It is a self-regulated attempt to right the feelings caused by being outside of the foundation, either to reduce the anger, fear, anxiety, or stress when the sympathetic system is hijacked, or to increase energy and raise oneself up out of the abyss of numbness, frozen affect, depression, or freeze associated with the dorsal vagal complex.

To nonaddicts, the idea that one could risk everything for a sexual thrill is insane, unfathomable, and very difficult to understand. "But he made choices!" we hear time and time again. Yes, he did, very poor choices made from a part of the brain that is not designed to make choices, only to react. I am not excusing unhealthy sexual behaviors any more than I would defend a drunk driver who injured someone; I am simply saying that while in active addiction, the part of the brain that is used to measure consequence and decision is offline. Once triggered, the old way of coping becomes the only avenue of choice.

In order to heal, the couple must understand that there are two foundations, two nervous systems operating and struggling through this crisis. It is imperative that the addict comes to know how his partner's nervous system has been affected by the discovery of his secret life, and he must learn to help regulate her system through being authentic, honest, transparent, and forthright in *everything* he does.

The Addiction Made Me Do It

While what is said in this book is completely based on fact regarding how the brain and nervous system work and how addiction is a brain disorder, addiction is *never* an excuse for bad behavior. Claiming that "it wasn't my fault; I have an addiction" will

1. invalidate the partner's pain;
2. cause all of the partner's defense systems to activate, taking her out of her foundation; and
3. give the understanding and treatment of sex addiction as a legitimate illness a bad name.

You, and you alone, are responsible for what you did, even though you were not doing it with the conscious brain. Similarly, an alcoholic who drives drunk and severely injures or kills another person while drunk did so in an altered state. However, even though the person is not responsible for being an alcoholic, he or she is absolutely responsible for any injury to others. Couples can and do heal from this illness and at times become more emotionally intimate than they could ever imagine. But there is a lot of work to be done, beginning with proper emotional regulation. To keep growing, there are certain truisms I have found that happen repeatedly. Adhering to the suggestions below will make long-term sobriety and recovery a reality and will also make the rebuilding of trust much more possible.

Knowing Her Foundation

In order to help your wife or partner heal, you must have an understanding of how your behaviors have permanently affected her nervous system and her ability to trust. You have just created an adverse developmental experience that will take months, if not years, to repair. Knowing your partner's foundation, her triggers, her reactions, and how she deals with these reactions will provide you with the opportunity to create safety. Your partner, like every other person on the planet, has experienced pain and wounds throughout her lifetime. Her discovery of your sexual betrayal has now lit on fire every other wound of a similar nature she has ever experienced. Most likely, immediately following discovery, your partner will be experiencing shock, numbness, fear, deep pain, and loss. After this brief period, she will swing to the other extreme and experience panic, anxiety, fear, and rage. She will become a detective, sometimes staying up for days at a time, searching for more evidence of betrayal. You will be bombarded with questions, and you will experience your own shock and fear by witnessing firsthand what your sexual addiction has created. You can help, and to do so you have to get out of yourself, your shame, your guilt, your self-loathing, and all the other selfish emotions you are having.

This is about her—her pain, her fear, and her crushed dreams. Focusing on how her pain affects you is selfish and narcissistic. Changing your behavior so you don't feel bad is about you, not about her. Shame is a worthless emotion that makes us focus on ourselves and what others think of us. Trying to manage her foundation is control, manipulation, and codependency. You are managing her foundation so you don't feel bad, not so she feels peace. You must first know and understand how you are reacting to her pain. In most cases everything you have been trying to avoid through your addiction, your insecurities, fear of abandonment, people pleasing, and your chameleonlike nature will be screaming for relief. You might have just realized your worst fear: if you really knew me, you'd reject me.

It is extremely important here and for the foreseeable future to quit making this about you. Your behaviors did this to you, your partner, your kids, your career, reputation, your life, *not* your personal worth. Knowing this will help you stay out of the pit of selfish emotions like shame and help you begin to focus on understanding, sharing and relieving her pain.

Knowing Your Foundation

Sex addiction is most likely the only addiction that creates more of what we are trying to avoid in the first place. You craved closeness but were afraid of what would happen if you let others in. When young, you were vulnerable and authentic and when you let others in, you were invaded, ignored, neglected, condemned, and shamed—so you stopped, you isolated, built a secret life, and became addicted to your own brain chemistry.

But, in the light of discovery, you are thrust into the awareness of what you've done. You become aware again of the longing for closeness and love, but now, your behaviors have caused the person with whom this was possible to be devastated, angry, crushed, and hurt. What you wanted most is now not available. Your behaviors have just ruined the connection you deeply craved.

If you want to get better, if you want to restore trust, then you have to take control of your recovery by working very hard to find, understand, and resolve the people, places, and events that caused you to be invulnerable and inauthentic in the first place. Like your partner, you have been subjected to devastating wounds that are now in the forefront of your mind. How you respond to these feelings makes all the difference in whether your relationship can survive.

You are now fully responsible for doing everything humanly possible to not only heal yourself but provide the stability your partner will need to recover.

Providing Stability

At this stage the addict is raw and tender *and* must be the stabilizing force in the relationship and home. I hear addicts' arguments all the time about "her" being partly to blame, or "She won't stop the questions," or "She is always angry."

First and foremost, tattoo on your eyelids, "She is not to blame." How she is reacting is caused by *you*. My usual response to complaints about the partner's defects is met with the question, "If it was so bad, why didn't you have the courage to leave?" Being stable, staying emotionally regulated, is the only way you will convince your partner that she can begin to trust you again.

Integrity, consistency, and repair are your only goals. Integrity means that from now on you are one person: authentic, rigorously honest, transparent, and accountable. There are no longer two of you; there is only one, and your partner has to see this every day for a long period of time to believe that this is the authentic you. This may be terrifying, but it is the only thing I have seen work to repair the damage caused by a life full of betrayal.

Also, you must know your partner's nervous system and her responses to the betrayal and the subsequent triggers that will occur. You must respond in a nondefensive, openly supportive way. Undoubtedly, you are filled with shame, remorse, self-loathing, and guilt with the exposure of your secret life. Wallowing in these emotions will do nothing to provide safety to your partner. They focus the attention back on you when all your attention must be focused on helping your partner's damaged emotions. You have to understand how the adverse developmental experience you have just created makes your partner respond. At times she will be numb and distant, and at other times she will be rageful, hyperaroused, questioning, and considering leaving.

It is incredibly important to allow her to have this experience and regain the power that your addiction has stolen from her. You will be afraid, insecure, and in need of reassurance, but your partner cannot do this for you. Whenever your partner is triggered, you must do as the stewardess instructs on every flight—put your own oxygen mask on before you can help others. You are now responsible not only for understanding and regulating your own nervous system but also for allowing your partner to feel, think, and believe whatever she deems necessary without defense, justification, or anger. When you manage your own system, your partner's unconscious nervous system will sense safety and stability. Your own recovery will do wonders for her recovery.

The Musts of Sobriety and Recovery

Alcoholics Anonymous has a saying that states, "The suggestions we make here are just that, suggestions. But these suggestions are the kind of suggestions like, I suggest you wear a parachute when you jump out of a plane."

My only goal here is to provide both the addict and the partner with a template for healing that I have found extremely successful *if followed*. This list was designed in my treatment programs to provide the addict with what is needed to stay away from relapse and to increase trust, whether the partner stays or leaves. If the addict is to get better and really heal, he will need to increase his authenticity and vulnerability on a daily basis. This work will continue the rest of his life and has no end point other than to become who he really is, who he was born to be, before any adverse development experiences changed him. The outline below is what an addict needs to do to increase his ability to be present for what the partner needs to heal.

Staying Present with the Partner's Experience

As discussed in the last chapter, you both will be walking through a minefield of triggers. The addict will be triggered from his unresolved ADEs that caused him to believe he was unworthy and unlovable. He will be filled with shame, and his most likely avenue at the start to defend himself will be to freeze, shut down, and withdraw.

The partner, on the other hand, once over the initial shock of discovery, will be filled with terror, pain, and rage. When navigating the minefield, it is always the addict's responsibility to ensure safe ground. He will lead and disarm the mines that are now scattered everywhere. In terms of using the foundation to describe how to navigate this painful time, the addict must come to learn and know *everything* that may trigger his partner, how she reacts when triggered, and what to do with the triggers to help her return to her frontal lobe and a semblance of safety.

To a triggered partner, the absolute worst thing an addict can do is shut down. The partner's brain and nervous system will read this as unsafe, dismissive, uncaring, and defensive. No matter what you are feeling, thinking, or believing at this moment, you *must* stay present. You can use ice, intense cardio, progressive relaxation, use your five senses, or name colors, but you must take the lead and provide safety by stabilizing your nervous system.

Following the principles below has proved successful not only in helping the addict stay sober but also in kick-starting the partner's healing.

Accountability

An important concept to remember here is that no matter how your partner is reacting right now, you caused it. When you get overwhelmed and want her to stop, or you go into blame, remember this: "My behaviors are what caused this reaction. I did this; I hurt you. I've lied, cheated, betrayed, destroyed your trust, hid from you, and was completely dishonest with you in every way."

Being accountable means you take full responsibility for the pain, damage, and emotions that are now occurring, without defense, without excuse. She doesn't want to hear "I'm sorry" over and over again. She wants to hear that you were wrong, that what you did was a mean, selfish, and dishonest way to treat someone whom you profess you love.

Staying out of Shame

Your shame is about you and has nothing to do with your partner. Shame is a self-focused response that leaves you feeling unworthy of connection. Shame takes you away from what your partner really needs, destroys empathy, and leaves your partner wondering how the focus got back on you. When my addict patient goes into shame in a couple's session, the partner immediately feels abandoned and frustrated because the addict is deflecting. Many addicts say, "I don't want to tell her" or "I can't stand seeing her in paid." My response to this is, "No, you can't stand feeling pain. It has nothing to do with her. Remember you have already hurt her. In most cases she just doesn't know it yet. Own the train wreck you've created. In this way, you and your partner can heal." Shame stops healing. When you find yourself in shame, know that it is a reaction of self-protection that will shut down healing on the spot.

Being Authentic

Stop lying in any form, whether an outright lie (no, I didn't do that) or lying by omission (well, if she doesn't ask just the right question, it's not a lie). Authenticity is the capacity to be fully you and share yourself 100 percent with your partner. Authenticity and integrity here are the same thing. There is one of you, and that you stays you all the time. No more masks, diversions, hiding, compartmentalizing, dishonesty, deceit, gaslighting, or pretending. Addicts become addicts because their authenticity was never valued in their early environments. This is not your early environment. If you are to heal from sex addiction and rebuild any trust, there must be authenticity all the time.

Being Transparent

In sexual addiction recovery, transparency means we don't keep secrets. We tell the truth about our sobriety and recovery, even if it means we will suffer consequences. With the couples in my practice, the lack of transparency has caused more damage than any other form of behavior. A simple "she doesn't need to know this" has set more than one partner back to square one and is absolutely enough to end a relationship or marriage.

Conversely, the patients that are absolutely transparent, while facing possible upset and hurt within their partner, usually are thanked for the honesty after the initial upset. The transparency includes anything: a text message, phone call, or e-mail from an old acting-out partner. A relapse with masturbation, pornography, massage parlor, or prostitute. Whatever the behavior, in true recovery these relapses must be admitted immediately.

Being Nondefensive

One of the most difficult things I see patients encounter is to remain nondefensive when seeing how much pain they have caused. It appears that the brain is automatically set to defend itself from pain. The minute the partner expresses her hurt, I often see the addict deny, argue, blame, ignore, excuse, avoid, stonewall, get angry, justify, or try to rationalize. Defensiveness creates feelings of being dismissed, of not being heard, of not being valuable or important.

Again, remember, you caused the pain, so why are you now trying to pretend that the pain isn't real? Joining her pain and validating her pain will help her heal; defending yourself will create more pain for her and ultimately for you. Brené Brown, when speaking of empathy, states that one of the elements of empathy is perspective taking. Working constantly on the ability to see how she was damaged by your behaviors and taking her perspective will help her heal.

I will leave you with what I call "the certainties" that I have seen every couple experience as they move through the healing process.

1. When things are calm, and you reestablish closeness, even for a few hours or a day, it will inevitably be followed by a time of distancing.
2. Your very presence will often trigger her.
3. She will be hurt and sad and will remain triggered for a very long time.
4. Your partner gets to have bad days. Trying to manipulate, control, or do sobriety for anyone but you will end very badly.
5. What she doesn't know *will* hurt her.

Glossary

agency: A sense of self-awareness; being in control of one's own life.

attunement: To be reactive and responsive to another person's needs and moods.

autonomic or emotional dysregulation: Emotional reactions that are not considered normal; mood swings.

avoidant attachment personality: When an infant does not seek proximity to a parent or caregiver after separation; the child is not affected when the parent leaves or returns.

brainspotting: A treatment method that works on identifying, processing, and releasing core neurophysiological sources of emotional/body pain, trauma, dissociation, and a variety of challenging symptoms.

cognitive dissonance: Mental stress experienced when a person holds two contradictory beliefs, ideas, or values.

downregulation: The brain's ability to regulate dopamine receptors.

EMDR (eye movement desensitization and reprocessing): A treatment that brings together traumatic memories and positive thoughts and beliefs to help reduce the distress stemming from a traumatic event.

neuroception: The brain's ability to sense safety.

polyvagal theory: A theory that specifies two functionally distinct branches of the vagus, or tenth cranial nerve.

PTSD (posttraumatic stress disorder): An anxiety disorder that develops after a person witnesses or experiences a traumatic event; can include flashbacks, nightmares, and uncontrollable thoughts about the experience.

regulation: Using a substance or behavior to cope with an adverse experience.

sensorimotor psychotherapy: Also known as "body-oriented talk therapy" to help clients to become aware of their bodies, to track their bodily sensations, and to implement physical actions that promote empowerment and competency.

social engagement system: A two-way interaction system that refers to a person's participation in a community or society.

somatic experiencing: A form of therapy aimed at relieving and resolving the symptoms of posttraumatic stress disorder (PTSD) and other mental and physical trauma-related health problems by focusing on the client's perceived body sensations.

tolerance: (1) The ability to tolerate stress in various forms without negative consequences; (2) an acceptance of the behavior, values, and beliefs of another person.

triune brain: The three layers of the brain that show its evolutionary growth: reptilian, limbic, and neocortex (frontal lobe).

References

AddictionHope.com. 2018. Sexual Addiction Causes, Statistics, Addiction Signs, Symptoms & Side Effects. Accessed January 8, 2018 https://www.addictionhope.com/sexual-addiction.

Anda, Robert F., Vincent J. Felitti, J. Douglas Bremner, John D Walker, Charles Whitfield, Bruce D. Perry, Shanta R. Dube and Wayne H. Giles (2006). The Enduring Effects of Abuse and Related Adverse Experiences in Childhood: A Convergence of Evidence from Neurobiology and Epidemiology. European Archives of Psychiatry and Clinical Neuroscience. 256. 174-186. 10.1007/s00406-005-0624-4..

APA (American Psychiatric Association). 2013. *Diagnostic and Statistical Manual of Mental Disorders*. 5th ed. Washington, DC: American Psychiatric Association.

ASAM (American Society of Addiction Medicine). 2017. "Public Policy Statement: Definition of Addiction." Accessed March 20. http://asam.org/for-the-public/definition-of-addiction.

Carleton, Jacqueline. 2012. "Pat Ogden: Pioneer of the Past, Wave of the Future." *Somatic Psychotherapy Today* (Summer). Accessed May 16, 2017. https://issuu.com/somaticpsychotherapytoday/docs/summer_2012_reduced_pdf/39.

Carnes, Patrick. 1992. *Don't Call It Love: Recovery from Sexual Addiction*. New York: Bantam Books.

———. 2001. *Out of the Shadows: Understanding Sexual Addiction*. Center City, MN: Hazelden.

Courtois, Christine. 2014. *It's Not You, It's What Happened to You*. Long Beach, CA: Elements Behavioral Health.

Domonoske, Camila. 2016. "Utah Declares Porn a Public Health Hazard." The Two-Way. National Public Radio. www.npr.org/sections/thetwo-way/2016/04/20/474943913/utah-declares-porn-a-public-health-hazard.

Goleman, Daniel. 2005. *Emotional Intelligence: Why It Can Matter More Than IQ.* New York: Bantam.

Hebb, Donald O. 1949. *The Organization of Behavior.* New York: Wiley & Sons.

Levine, Peter. 2008. *Healing Trauma.* Boulder, CO: Sounds True.

———. 2010. "Peter Levine on Somatic Experiencing." Interview by Victor Yalom and Marie-Helene Yalom. Psychotherapy.net. April 2010. Accessed May 21, 2017. http://www.psychotherapy.net/interview/interview-peter-levine#section-emotional-processing-with-trauma-survivors.

MacLean, Paul D. 1990. *The Triune Brain in Evolution.* New York: Plenum Press.

Maté, Gabor. 2000. *Scattered Minds: The Origins and Healing of Attention Deficit Disorder.* Canada: Vintage Ontario.

———. 2010. *In the Realm of Hungry Ghosts: Close Encounters with Addiction.* Berkeley, CA: North Atlantic Books.

Miller, Alice. 2009. *Breaking Down the Wall of Silence: The Liberating Experience of Facing Painful Truth.* New York: Basic Books.

Ogden, Pat, and Janina Fisher. 2015. *Sensorimotor Psychotherapy: Interventions for Trauma and Attachment.* New York: W. W. Norton.

Perry, Bruce D., and Ronnie Pollard. 1997. "Altered Brain Development Following Global Neglect in Early Childhood." *Society for Neuroscience: Proceedings from Annual Meeting.* New Orleans.

Perry, Bruce D., R. Pollard, Toi L. Blaicley, William L. Baker, Domenico Vigilante.. 1995. "Childhood Trauma, the Neurobiology of Adaptation and 'Use-Dependent' Development of the Brain: How 'States' Become 'Traits.'" *Infant Mental Health Journal* 16 (4): 273.

R. F. Anda, V. J. Felitti, J. D. Bremner, J. D. Walker, Ch. Whitfield, B. D. Perry, Sh. R. Dube, W. H. Giles. 2006. "The Enduring Effects of Abuse and Related Adverse Experiences in Childhood: A Convergence of Evidence from Neurobiology and Epidemiology." *European Archives of Psychiatry and Clinical Neuroscience* 256 (3): 174–86. Accessed May 21, 2017. https://link.springer.com/article/10.1007/s00406-005-0624-4

Porges, Stephen. 2011. *The Polyvagal Theory: Neurophysiological Foundations of Emotions, Attachment, Communication, and Self-Regulation.* New York: Norton.

Scaer, Robert. 2007. *The Body Bears the Burden: Trauma, Dissociation and Disease.* Binghamton, NY: Haworth Press.

Sensorimotor Institute. n.d. "Trauma and The Body: The Theory and Practice of Sensorimotor Psychotherapy." Accesses January 12, 2018. https://www.sensorimotorpsychotherapy.org/Los_Angeles_Intro_WS_10_28_16.pdf

Siegel, Daniel. 2017. "Interview with Daniel Siegel, MD." By Cynthia Levin. AMHC.

Accessed May 19. http://amhc.org/poc/view_doc.php?type=doc&id=818.

Steffens, Barbara, and Marsha Means. 2009. *Your Sexually Addicted Spouse: How Partners Can Cope and Heal.* Liberty Corner, NJ: New Horizon Press.

Steffens, Barbara, and R. Rennie. 2006. "The Traumatic Nature of Disclosure for Wives of Sexual Addicts." *Sexual Addiction and Compulsivity* 13 (2–3): 247–67.

Van der Kolk, Bessel. 1994. Review. "The Body Keeps the Score: Memory and the Evolving Psychobiology of Posttraumatic Stress." *Harvard Review of Psychiatry.* 1(5): 253–65.

————. 2014. *The Body Keeps the Score: Brain, Mind, and Body in the Healing of Trauma.* New York: Penguin Books.

Weiss, Robert. 2015a. *Sex Addiction 101: A Basic Guide to Healing from Sex, Porn, and Love Addiction.* Deerfield Beach, FL: Health Communications.

————. 2015b. "Defining and Understanding the Cycle of Sexual Addiction." *Sex Addiction Expert Blogs*, January 20. Accessed April 17, 2017. https://www.addiction.com/expert-blogs/defining-understanding-cycle-sexual-addiction.

Wilson, Gary. 2014. *Your Brain on Porn.* United Kingdom: Commonwealth Publishing.

About the Author

Michael Barta, Ph.D., LPC., CSAT-S is the founder of the Colorado Sexual Recovery Center and the Begin Again Institute in Boulder, Colorado. Dr. Barta is a master clinician and a nationally-recognized speaker and author on the topic of sex and pornography addictions. For the past 10 years, he has guided his treatment centers while studying and creating a revolutionary model for the treatment of sexual addiction using the most recent findings from the world's leading neurological experts.

In 2015, Dr. Barta officially trademarked his theory and treatment modality known as Trauma Induced Sexual Addiction (TINSA®).